When Hope Hides

By Judith Bond Maddock

D1525001

ISBN 9798397309806
Independently published

2023

Cover photo by Ron Smith on Unsplash

Table of Contents

Acknowledgements

I've always known that I would author a book, but could never have anticipated that multiple child loss would be the subject matter of my memoir. Still, life has called me to fulfill what I sincerely believe is my soul's earthly purpose. Unfortunately, this came at an unfathomable price: the deaths of my sons John Ryan, Joshua, and Jeffrey. This memoir will have been worth every tear, every sleepless night, and all the buried thoughts and visions it reawakened if it helps bring even one person affected by child loss to a place of encouragement and hope.

When Hope Hides has come to fruition because of the support and help of many. I first must thank my three beautiful sons, whose stories are honorable and deserve to be told. They are forever with me and continue to bless me each day with their individual gifts of courage, resiliency, and acceptance. No words can express my gratitude for these children who have broken and opened up my heart, making it possible to share with you, my readers, their gifts of goodness and hope.

Thank you to my husband, John, the love and support of my life, who recognized and respected my need to have the space and massive amounts of time needed to bring this book to life for over three precious years of our life together. He has put up with the chaos of three different writing stations scattered throughout our home, my favorite being the island in our kitchen. He has been a silent support, and his presence has not gone unnoticed.

Thank you to my daughters Ondrea and Elizabeth, who have been searching for their own acceptance of the loss of three brothers. With each death, they courageously witnessed their mother fall to the depths of despair, only to come back up reassembled and changed by child loss. I will forever regret that they had to experience the impact of that in their mother, but I am eternally grateful for the support and stability they provided when I needed it most.

Thank you to my sister Nancy, lifelong guardian of my soul. She has been there for me in the worst and best of times. And thank you also to my mother Rose, who provides me with spiritual strength from above and who showed me how to love, lose, and go on.

Thank you to my personal hope holders Mary and Sandy, who gave me unlimited time and support with unending patience through the most brutal times of self-doubt and sadness. I will forever be thankful for your friendship.

Thank you to Tracy, my kind and knowledgeable tech assistant, who gave of her time and talents whenever I was in a panic or needed help coordinating revisions with my editor. I learned and quickly forgot foreign techy terms like "directories" and "mark-ups". And thank you to my editor Anne and book designer Pat who have believed in my story and brought it to life in book form at last.

To my dear friends Vicki Schmidt, Faith Simonson, Jim Johnson, Jenifer Hanson Shivers, Patrice Peterson, and Mary Karkela, who agreed to dredge through my "rough" rough draft and encouraged me when completing my book seemed like a far-off vision. And to Jane Dolan, at the local copy center, who patiently printed and reprinted copies of my manuscript so I could edit, revise, and create new drafts to be reprint-ed. She was the preserver of the treasured words and memories I held within.

To so many others who never gave up on me and continually cheered on my efforts and showed interest and support in my heart's huge en-deavor, thank you for holding me accountable when I doubted myself.

Judi Maddock

Preface

Late in my teens, I was offered a slight glimpse into my future as a mother. I had a message, a feeling, that led me to believe my years as a mother would be both purposeful and amazing. I also felt a forewarning or hint of some undefined challenge that lay ahead. I never gave it much thought and tucked it away in the back of my mind. While I was pregnant for the first time, this thought skipped through my thoughts again, and its voice had picked up a little volume. It retreated after the birth of my two healthy daughters, and it hid away as a whisper in my soul.

Never in a million years did I think the message meant I would lose all three of my sons. But that is my story. This memoir is truly a courageous work of my heart. It has required a hard and difficult remembrance and retelling of one mother's true story, one I would never have chosen. Writing this book has forced me to revisit difficult parts of my past. In some strange way it has become a cathartic vessel allowing me to challenge myself to look once more through the window of dark inner pain.

First, I believe I have been spiritually called to honor the life stories of each of our three beautiful sons who have died and to honor our two incredible daughters, Elizabeth and Ondrea. They remain my shining lights.

Secondly, my goal is to offer support to others who share the difficult journey of child loss. Through my story, I desire to bring them a message of hope for eventual acceptance and a return of joy. May these words from a mother's heart help you breathe in new life and give you the courage to look, if just for a minute, toward the light and inhale again. It is possible for a heart to survive after it has been dismantled by loss. Our scars will forever remain, although through dedicated work and the working of time, we can realize and find comfort that our hope has never really left. Rather, lost hope hides in the universe and is held in the hands of God, in the very loved one we grieve, and by those special people who support us with love and compassion. These are our hope holders.

My humble aspiration is that these words can serve as a bridge of encouragement, leading readers to find hope that hides. May these words from my heart be a healing balm for souls who walk in similar pain.

This is Hope

Nina Salaman

I knew a bird once in a far-off Spring

It sang and sang as though it would not die

For very love of living; but it died,

And all the trees in the gardens round

Heard it no more. And still within my heart

It sings and sings as though it could not die;

And thus, it lives—and so one's self shall live

Among all things rememb'ring. This is hope.

Part One

JOHN RYAN MADDOCK

You gain strength, courage, and confidence by every experience in which you really stop to look fear in the face. You are able to say to yourself 'I lived through this horror. I can take the next thing that comes along. You must do the thing you think you cannot do.

Eleanor Roosevelt

On July 22, 1976, we arrived at the hospital for what would be my third and final C-section. While being prepped for surgery, I was thrilled with anticipation at seeing our family's newest little member. In the operating room, I observed the hustle and bustle and hum of cheerful chatter. My masked obstetrician poked his head over my surgical draping to ask whether I was ready to see what nine months of waiting had in store for me. My spinal had been administered, and the surgical team began to move in sync to bring our new baby into the world. Because this was not my first rodeo, I knew that the baby would be quickly retrieved. Within minutes, a nurse happily announced that a little boy had arrived.

I was thrilled that he was here at last—but quickly sensed that they were hovering over my son. Their muffled voices raised fearful concerns within me. When they brought him closer towards me, it was obvious that my precious baby showed signs of labored breathing. A nurse explained away his rapid breathing as a phenomenon that is sometimes present in newborns and not to worry. To assess him more fully, they whisked away this tightly swaddled bundle through the operating room doors toward the nursery.

My pregnancy had been normal, and my nausea had been minimal this time around. I had done all the right and healthy things in preparation for this moment. Even so, my mind recalled the unease and foreboding buried deep in my memory, unsettling and haunting my thoughts. Now I found myself desperately denying their existence. In a panic, I waited for some kind of reassurance from the surgical team. Everything is fine, I thought. It has to be.

But it wasn't. The medical team was concerned about the continued inability of our newborn's little body to self-regulate his rapid breathing. Things began taking a more serious turn. I had talked before the arrival of the baby with our daughters' pediatrician in a larger hospital system across town. I had shared with him that in the event of problems, we would want our baby transported to St. Luke's Neonatal Unit. Looking back, I must have been giving some subconscious credence to my longtime premonition. In addition, I was never one to take the miracle of birth for granted. The hospital where John Ryan was born did not have an official neonatal unit—only a small room off the nursery with a couple of isolettes and a curtain that could be drawn to provide very minimal privacy for medical staff, parents, and their struggling newborns.

The decision was made to immediately transfer our fragile newborn by ambulance to St. Luke's Hospital. I read the concern in John's eyes as he checked in before accompanying our baby to the ICU that was awaiting John Ryan's arrival. Was there something my husband wasn't telling me? The brief moments when I had actually gotten to hold our sweet baby seemed forever molded into me. He had fit into my arms so perfectly and now they yearned for him.

While I recovered from my C-section in the hospital, John updated me frequently about how our little guy was doing. I thanked God for each new day that brought me moments closer to our reunion. Throughout the day I tried to picture John Ryan's precious little face. There had been no opportunity for pictures or for studying him closely. Our meeting was painfully brief. My eyes created a river of tears as my body and mind agonized over our separation. I tried to put on a brave face and remember what I knew in my heart: My baby was where he needed to be for now.

Early in the morning the day after John Ryan was born, I heard the sound of my obstetrician's voice in the hallway. When he popped in to check on me, he seemed utterly oblivious to the fact that the baby he had surgically removed from my uterus was now fighting for his life at a hospital across town. I kept waiting for an inkling of acknowledgement, but there was not a mention of my beautiful baby or his obvious condition at birth. It was a very awkward conversation. Did he seriously not know what trauma was pulling at this patient's every breath? I was at a loss for words and could not enter easily into the two-way conversation he was eagerly trying to generate. As he turned and left the room, he poked his head back in the doorway and proceeded to slap my pain one more time by telling a lousy joke with an even more pitiful punch line. A stand-up comedian he was not. His insensitivity was hurtful, and I found myself disappointed and embarrassed by his lack of compassion and professionalism.

I continued to progress well physically. As if on cue, on day three I became a human milking machine. John was teased by the nurses at both hospitals about his newfound role as a milk man, as daily he picked up and delivered a new supply across town to the other hospital. I produced such an abundance of milk that I thought perhaps I could give it away to another needy infant. Unfortunately, in those days, that thought was quickly banished as absurd and laughable. Thus, the pump and pour operation continued in full gear.

On the fifth day I was discharged, and within 20 minutes I was riding the elevator up to St. Luke's neonatal unit to reunite with my sweet baby. I already knew that John Ryan's journey over the past several days had been nothing less than a nightmarish roller coaster. Not being with him only added to my distress. I was ushered off the elevator into a section of the hospital nursery that new moms never want to see. I was led over to the isolette which held my still-struggling little man. Looking through its clear plastic window, featuring a small hole for access by neonatal nurses and doctors, my hands yearned to touch him. I remember drinking in his little face and the whole of him, as his body heaved with every breath. Tubes and patches adorned his frail little body. The tears that washed over my eyes created a protective veil from the raw and naked reality that lay before me.

The days that followed were filled with beeping isolettes and noisy machines in the small, crowded nursery of critically ill infants. Each beautiful new creation was fighting its own fight. Because John Ryan was too medically fragile to be removed from the isolette and held, I sought out the nursery's rocking chair and moved it up close to my baby. Its comforting rhythmic motion calmed me. So did St. Luke's first-ever neonatal pediatric cardiologist, whose kind manner and presence were very welcome. His caring hands and knowledge now held all our hope, and he quickly became a human version of Superman in our eyes.

Many tests were discussed and orders made. It was evident that our baby was racing against the clock. We had been launched into a foreign land and were in no way prepared for what this mysterious unknown path might reveal. We were thankful for the highly skilled ICU nurses who were so gentle and loving in their care of our baby and the other infants in their care. Each evening before leaving our son, we were reassured knowing that we would be promptly informed of any concerning changes that might be detected in our absence. I remember making many calls in the middle of the night just to make sure that the luxury of a few hours of restorative sleep was justified and that all was status quo with our baby. We were mentally and physically drained, so mornings were jarring and always came too quickly. We would grab a cup of coffee, get our girls situated with family, and rush off to experience another day of cautious hope, as minute-by-minute John Ryan's medical situation darted randomly in different directions. We attempted to piece together every event that unfolded, hoping that when joined together they might provide important clues to John Ryan's chances for improvement and survival. Often, the reports that greeted us left us with a lump in our throats and a pounding in our hearts that seemed audible to the outside world. It was a constant one step forward, two steps back dance, and it was physically and emotionally challenging.

Due to John Ryan's impaired heart, our baby lacked an adequate sucking reflex. Because of that, he had a difficult time ingesting milk and an even harder time holding it down. This was the key hurdle for our son, who was having trouble getting the nourishment he needed to build his strength. And it was the lack of nourishment that was throwing a wrench into our baby's harrowing fight for life. One day in the neonatal floor led into weeks. One particular morning we were led into a small room to meet with doctors. John Ryan had been through a particularly difficult night and his valiant little body was struggling beyond its capacity. Overnight ultrasounds had shown some valve repairs were needed in the right chamber of his heart. Though our baby was so very weak, the cardiologists felt it was crucial to proceed, and promptly our fears became true. Time had run out. Waiting was no longer an option, nor was transferring him to a larger surgical center in the Minneapolis/St. Paul area. As I gazed into this tiny, courageous face and watched my baby's tiny chest heave in frantic gasps to capture air, I knew we had no other choice. With tears, soft touches, words of love, and uncountable prayers for his safety, we released him into the hands of competent doctors who would apply their knowledge in an attempt to correct his abnormalities and help his minuscule heart function more efficiently. This was his only hope and ours for any chance to keep him with us.

Family was called, and we gathered in the ICU waiting room for what seemed like forever. Praying, pacing like caged animals, and downing too many Styrofoam cups of overheated coffee, we searched the faces of every medical staff person that passed for some indication of hope to float our hearts. The halls were empty, and there was no sign of activity, making it the perfect time to gather with my sister in the nearby restroom for a quick bathroom break from reality and a lipstick application. I felt safe and secluded, when suddenly a pounding on the bathroom door ended our temporary escape. Herded into the hallway, we looked down past a long narrow space lined with doors. I focused on what appeared to be nurses pushing a larger fully enclosed isolette. Following closely behind were doctors and someone calling "Clear the halls! Clear the halls!" As they approached, I spotted our brave little fighter.

My heart was overwhelmed with pride for my little son's enormous courage to battle through a delicate and risky surgery with slim odds.

It felt like every life celebration wrapped up in one— and as if I had just received the greatest gift of all, beautifully wrapped anew in shimmering hope, the very life of my child. It was truly a shining moment that will live in my memory forever. The fact that he was able to hang on through hours of delicate surgery was a remarkably huge tribute to the most courageous little fighter I will ever know. The strong life force dwelling deep within John Ryan's frail body must have whispered him through those tenuous hours of fragile surgery. This was the very first open-heart surgery on a small and critically ill infant at this hospital. The surgeon was highly regarded by patients and staff. A man of great faith and humility, he had prayed with his team for God's help before John Ryan's surgery started. My heart was in my throat as I watched our little hero rushed past us and toward the ICU. Tears of joyful relief ran down our faces, realizing the miracle of our little boy being gifted with a new chance at life.

Our family huddled together nervously in the family waiting room as he was settled into his ICU room. He had entered an extremely critical time of post-surgical recovery. We tried to remain on guard, protecting our racing hearts while trying to ready them for any possible outcome. Gratitude cut through my anxiety as I relived over and over again that miraculous moment of pride for a son with courage bigger than he was. My forever little hero.

When we were allowed into the ICU, seeing him hooked up to a menagerie of tubes and machines was overwhelming. The equipment overshadowed his tiny body. As I watched my baby continue to struggle toward a better life, I noticed that his breathing was still very labored. His occasional cries were trying to come to the surface through his swollen vocal cords, irritated by the many intubations. He drew his little knees up toward his chest, and I felt helpless to bring him comfort from outside the plexiglass barrier. John Ryan's nurse kindly reminded me that his little body was fighting to maximum capacity and that he had been amazingly tolerant in post-surgery, so far requiring minimal pain medication. I stared at him trying to absorb what I had been told. My beautiful boy, valiant and determined to cling to life with such tenacity.

We retreated to our second home in the ICU family room to wait things out. John and I were both thrilled that doctors had been able to do some valve repair on the right chamber of his heart, but they reminded us that John Ryan remained in extremely critical condition. His status was very much touch and go, and we would require every prayer of hope for survival that we and others could send him. It was not an easy time. We slept on the couches, one of us each night—usually John, since I had still not healed completely from my own major surgery. With a lot of help from family, we were able to be in the hospital nearly every moment.

One afternoon, I was in the ICU room with John Ryan when alarms on his machines started beeping and blaring. Nurses came running from every direction. I was told to leave. They were about to call a code on our baby. I was close to hysterical as I shared the news with John in the family waiting room. We could see his pediatrician and cardiology doctors literally sprinting down the hallway toward the Intensive Care Unit. The code was repeated as blinking lights in the hallways accentuated the urgency of this event. It was the scariest moment of my life so far. I found myself wondering if this was how John Ryan's triumphant short life would end.

Eventually a nurse came and told us that John Ryan had quit breathing and that fortunately they were able to resuscitate him. Once again, we were lulled into a state of cautious gratitude. We rode this unpredictable roller coaster for the next few weeks as John Ryan endured other critical moments. Over time, he stabilized enough to return to neonatal nursery. The familiarity of the neonatal nurses and its surroundings awarded us a wee bit more comfort. However, the uncertainty continued. From hour to hour and day to day, we never knew if we would be met with a comforting smile or a look of concern. We craved the return to some kind of normalcy.

After nearly six tumultuous weeks, we were told that John Ryan was ready to go home with us. As much as I had dreamed for this day, questions and fears immediately flooded my mind. There was so much to learn about his care, and I wanted to be sure I knew how to handle any medical emergency that might arise. Nurses were kind but dismissive when I asked for a home monitor and a demonstration on resuscitating our baby. I was assured that these measures were not necessary, because John Ryan's progress would be monitored by frequent follow-up clinic appointments. Leaving the hospital with a long list of instructions and our miniscule baby tucked into a monstrous infant seat. We were excited and overwhelmed. In the elevator, we were met by a kind face who John soon recognized as his childhood friend's mother. She wanted a peek at our little guy, who was sleeping soundly in his infant seat surrounded by a big yellow blanket that accentuated his tiny body. Tears rolled down her face as she shared how her own infant did not survive a serious heart ailment. Saying goodbye when we reached the main floor, she wished us good luck and happiness. I will never forget the pain I saw in her face and how it touched me.

John Ryan's darling nursery had been set up with an air of comfortable expectation. Pale blue walls and crisp white curtains hung in waiting. The comforter covering his blue crib was lined with yellow bumper pads and an eye-catching red and white gingham checked zip-up comforter. We had purchased the sweetest crib mobile. With five yellow ducks that circulated round and round to the tune of "Playmate Come Out and Play with Me", it would make for a mesmerizing view for baby. In the corner, my small wooden childhood rocker sat waiting. Everything was ready for our brave little prince's homecoming.

In the days that followed, I tried so hard to give our new little one and ourselves a routine that instilled normalcy. I wanted with all my might to treat my baby with the same mothering I had given my girls. But I knew deep down that this baby would require a different recipe of care than the regimen of care given to our two healthy newborns. We limited visitors due to our baby's extreme vulnerability to outside germs and illness. I was painfully aware of the reactions of those who came by to view John Ryan. The usual pleas to hold and admire him were noticeably absent. Instead, there were looks of concern and compassionate sadness as visitors cast their eyes on his beautiful face and tiny, frail body. Instead of showing happiness for the miracle of John Ryan—and alleviating some of our worry and concern—the onlookers' faces only reflected our fears and reaffirmed our buried sadness.

I remember vividly the beautiful September day I packed up the girls and John Ryan for an afternoon visit to Grandma Rose's house across the river in Moorhead. The girls greeted their grandma and raced through the house to the large tree-covered back yard. I handed John

Ryan to his grandma and grabbed a freshly brewed cup of coffee. We watched our giggly girls perform their tumbling acts. John Ryan slept blissfully in Grandma Rose's arms while she carefully scrutinized him. I tried to avoid locking eyes with her, because I knew she was about to tell me what I didn't want to hear. I deeply valued my mother's opinion, but at that moment I didn't have the inner strength to hear it. True to herself, Mom looked at me and said, "I don't know... he just doesn't look right." Her brutally honest words cut to the very quick of my heart, because they mirrored my unspoken thoughts exactly

Emotionally exhausting days continued with pumping and pouring breast milk into sterilized bottles and visiting the pediatrician for progress and discouraging weight check-ins. Each visit magnified my frustration and fears concerning his inability to gain the weight and strength he needed. I wanted so much to breastfeed my baby, but John Ryan's weak sucking reflex continued to not allow that. Each ounce of breast milk I successfully fed him by bottle was a celebration in my mind. Disappointingly, John Ryan's body almost immediately rejected it, and we found ourselves back at square one. One feeding cycle seemed to go on forever, and usually ended in him falling asleep and me feeling I'd failed again. It didn't matter how I held him, what nipple or bottle I used, who held it, how many burps could be brought up, or how many lullabies were sung. The end result was always the same. More milk came out than stayed in. Behind my failing efforts stood a supportive husband, two beautiful little girls who needed mommy time too, and a self-blaming mom with a sleeping baby who desperately needed to gain weight. But John and I remained steadfast 24 hours a day, day in and day out. Sleep happened only in fits and starts. It was easy to perceive that John Ryan was uncomfortable most of the time, and the rocking chair became our friend as its rhythmic movement offered some comfort. Looking at that adorable little face of courage gave me the strength I needed to stay strong for the miracle in my arms.

Since the girls had gone back to school in the fall, mornings had become treasured time alone with John Ryan. Before long, the girls would come bouncing through the back door for a hug and a quick lunch before Elizabeth met up with her friends to return to school and first grade. Ondrea was in half-day kindergarten and home in the afternoons with me and her brother.

While our family life was slowly settling back into a rhythm of sorts, pumping and pouring my breast milk into sterilized bottles continued along with exhausting, frequent, and less-than-encouraging weigh-ins at the clinic. He was getting older, but his weight was in a stagnant holding pattern.

My favorite time alone with John Ryan was when I gave him his daily tubby in the kitchen sink. These precious bathing times felt so normal. Gazing into John Ryan's steely blue eyes, my hope was recharged. He seemed to find the warm water soothing too. His fuzzy light brown baby hair was growing back into the spots that had been shaved in the ICU for tubes and sensors. I loved washing him with Johnson and Johnson baby soap in the pink-and-white box and smearing him with after-bath lotion from the pink Mennen Baby Magic bottle. The familiar baby scents provided me sweet comfort and fleeting moments of nostalgia and normalcy. But his daily heart medication and medicine, phenobarbital, and medication to relieve acid reflux discomfort were constant reminders of his weakness. The surgical chest scar that took up most of his little torso had healed nicely. Each time I glanced at it, I was amazed all over again by my baby's fighting determination to live.

And so the weeks crept by. Because John Ryan required frequent feedings around the clock, quality sleep was not a realistic option. When I could sleep, I would wake up startled and worried if I hadn't heard him stirring within a comfortable period of time. His cry was still weak and raspy. Looking back, when we finally exited through those hospital doors with our new baby in hand, we could never have known the complexity and intensity our caregiving would demand or the journey that lay ahead.

Eventually, his doctor gave me the okay to switch him to a special soy formula to see if he would tolerate that better. Unfortunately, the change didn't make a difference. In many ways, John Ryan was a typical heart baby, small for his age and frequently uncomfortable. Even though we were continually running into walls trying to find a solution to his feeding difficulties, we never gave up hope that he would grow out of them. Nonetheless, feeding difficulties and minimal weight gains remained the primary concern in his progress and survival. I desperately wanted to believe that our baby was repaired now and that everything would eventually follow an easier path and feel less hopeless. I know that a mother's love for her child is often superhuman, and sometimes I think I convinced myself that I had the power to think my thoughts and wishes for John Ryan into reality. Any small sign of improvement became a huge leap in my forlorn mind. I needed to fan the fire of hope somehow. Our girls continued to create smiles through priceless pictures and endearing cards. They brought some normal back into our lives during abnormal conditions.

We decided to move ahead with our decision to have John Ryan circumcised. Perhaps this rite of passage would provide an added sense of permanence in this world for our baby. John and I had considered all the science and cultural norms and concluded that it was the right thing to do for our son. Armed with a medical okay, we scheduled the procedure to be done in the clinic.

In the waiting room, a feeling built up inside me. I wanted to bolt out of the clinic with John Ryan and never look back. Maybe we were wrong, and there were hidden dangers we hadn't recognized. I could still change my mind! Soon after, John Ryan's name was called, and we followed a nurse into a small procedural room. The nurse's calming manner helped, but the panic must have remained in my eyes. I reluctantly transferred my baby to her waiting arms. She reassured me that they would apply a numbing substance and that the pain would be minimal. Back in the waiting room, I was bombarded with tremendous pangs of guilt. What had we been thinking? How could I add more pain to his struggle? When a nurse appeared before me and led me back to my baby. I only wanted to hold him close and tell him I was sorry. I could tell that the procedure had taken a lot out of him. He slept all the way home, his little cheeks moving to the beat of his pacifier, and when he did remarkably better than I had feared he might, I forgave myself after a few weeks had passed.

Sunday morning, October 24, 1976, John Ryan was more irritable and even more resistant to digesting formula. No matter how much we walked, rocked and sang to him or massaged his gaseous little belly, he continuously cried with discomfort. I felt inadequate and utterly helpless. The pediatrician who was on call prescribed something to help settle his indigestion down, and eventually, through his tears and mine, he was lulled into a short period of sleep. Red flags were waving inside me. John Ryan's body had never before shown such intense and unrelenting discomfort. Fear and panic consumed me. I didn't dare share my thoughts and feelings with John. What if saying them aloud made them real? I couldn't take that chance.

The day dragged on into the evening, with very minimal change. John and the girls had finally gone to bed, and I thought I could detect some response to the medication in John Ryan, and that allowed me to dare to breathe normally again. But our relief didn't last. Together we rocked and cuddled through another fitful several hours. I needed John to take over for a little while so I could rest my eyes. When I walked into the bedroom, John got himself fully dressed before taking our unsettled little baby into his arms. I remember finding that odd, but when my head hit the pillow I fell fast asleep.

At about 5:45 am I was awakened from a deep sleep by a powerful jolt from within my body. My feet hit the floor and I raced into the living room. I was relieved to see that John was sleeping on the couch with John Ryan snuggled upon his chest. They looked so peaceful together. But on closer inspection, I detected a strange stillness in my baby's breathing. John Ryan displayed a daunting blue ring around his tiny mouth. Screaming, I snatched my baby's limp body off John's chest and began to try every technique I could think of to get my baby boy to breathe again, including breathing into his open little mouth. But despite my efforts, John Ryan's tiny body felt limp and motionless in my arms.

John had called the ambulance and his parents to come and stay with the girls. We were both in tears as we continued our futile efforts to revive him. There was no visible sign of John Ryan's breath returning. While shock and fear overtook us, in the chaos our girls had come down from their bedroom to see what all the racket was about. Though John and I were all consumed with our lifeless child, I remember out of the corner of my eye seeing the girls entertaining themselves by bumping down the stairway on their bottoms and giggling wildly. This was how they were choosing to cope with their own fear.

The ambulance took forever to arrive. I raced out the front door and ran frantically to the nearby corner. I wanted more than anything to see or hear some sign that help was on the way. Someone had to do something to save our precious boy. Having no luck, I raced back inside to see John standing up with our lifeless baby a limp rag doll in his arms. He grabbed a blanket and holding John Ryan raced by me out the door toward our car. I felt my breath leave my lungs like deflating balloons. How could this be happening? I also knew that John Ryan's window for resuscitation was about to slam shut forever as we continued to wait for the paramedics to show.

The race to get to the hospital remains a blur in my husband's mind to this day. Waiting for my mother-in-law Helen to arrive seemed to take forever too, though I'm sure all of this frantic activity happened in just few minutes. However, in trauma there is only slow motion. When Helen pulled up, I jumped in the old tan station wagon as my sister-in-law Sheila jumped out to take care of the girls. At the hospital, I shot out of the car and into the ER. I had not heard from John since he ran past me with our son. I was scared to death to read their faces and imagined the worst. I could see everyone was still waiting for some word about John Ryan. My father-in-law Bernie had come to wait with John. My mom and stepdad Morris were on their way.

Suddenly John Ryan's pediatric cardiologist ran into the ER. His heavy parka flew through the air and landed on a nearby hook as he raced through the waiting room. He had a grave look on his face and his eyes were focused straight ahead. I couldn't help but remember how many times I had teased him about me showing up on his doorstep or calling him in the middle of the night in case of emergency. Sometimes in order to get a little alone time with my fear, I would drive by his homey gray two-story house nestled in a quiet cul-de-sac just a few miles north of my home. Knowing he was there comforted me.

Footsteps brought me back to reality. Precious seconds turned into minutes. My mind seemed to have vacated my body, which was in full-on hyper-vigilant mode. With the harrowing wait came the blatant thought that indeed things were not headed in a positive direction. But that was my head talking. My heart was telling me not to give up and to keep praying through my tears as I sat on the edge of a hard and unwelcoming chair.

In a trance, I was jarred by the sudden presence of a brown-haired lady with a badge. She crouched down alongside me, identifying herself as a hospital social worker and requested that we all follow her into a dimly lit family room. John and I sat at a table, the rest of our family surrounding us against the walls. My heart was closing in on me just like the walls. Every bit of available air was being sucked out of the room. Suddenly, our son's doctor came in and took a seat in the chair across from us. "I'm sorry," he said.

I slammed my fists down hard yelling "NO! NO!" and melted onto the table in a heap of inarticulate moaning and rage. Through my vocal chords rushed an uncontrollable howl. I sounded like dying prey. Through his own tears, the doctor reassured us that everything possible had been done to bring John Ryan back, and that they had worked to save him for over an hour. My mind was stunned. I wanted to never lift my head off that table.

No person is ever prepared for the words "your child is dead". It is not possible to measure the destruction and massacre of the heart triggered by those words. Nothing could have ever gotten me ready for this moment of bleak finality. I was, in that one moment, changed forever. It was the funeral before the funeral.

All of my prayers were now unanswered, my hopes for the future dashed, and my dreams slayed by two simple words: I'm sorry. How could our courageous little boy have lost his fight, and WHY? He had been in my arms just hours before, and now I would never hold him again. My child and I were a love team with a bond that had been violently shredded. I was breathing, so I knew I was alive, yet I felt out of touch with my physical self. My soul had suffered a simply unimaginable blow. I was left with a raw and irreparable wound that only a mother who loses a child knows. I remember wanting only to hold my two girls in my arms. Beyond that I knew nothing. My world had gone dark.

I don't remember much about leaving that chair in the ER family room, but I do know that John went with his dad and I rode with my mom and stepdad to their home. I remember floating from room to room through Mom's beautiful home and wondering what would happen if I stopped moving. I was afraid to find out.

Soon after, there was a knock on my mom's door. A prescription for tranquilizers had mysteriously been delivered in my name. This was not out of the ordinary in the 1970s, when tranquilizers were prescribed to those who had suffered a traumatic event as a way to numb overwhelming emotions thought too painful to bear. Child loss had apparently qualified me. I had never taken a medication like this before, and I was very reluctant. However, when I realized that I was having to remind myself to breathe, I agreed to take half a tablet, giving the other half to my mom. Within minutes, I felt numbed, somewhat detached and less reactive to the horrible events of the day, but I didn't like the powerful punch this small dose had delivered. I would not be a willing candidate for sedatives again.

Elizabeth, Ondrea, and John arrived at my mom's. It was comforting to have my little family reunited again. They were my world and my everything. It felt so right to be together and so wrong to be apart. Then my sister came through the back door and ran straight towards me. We became an entangled web of emotions and tears. We had shared so many family losses together, but none more devastating to me than this one. The day moved into dusk, and the thought of the cold, dark night made me afraid of the thought of closing my eyes. My mom suggested that we spend the night. I think she realized how difficult it would be for us to return home after all that had happened there earlier in the day. The girls were happy to be tucked in down the hall from Grandma and Grandpa. They loved staying in the room with brown wallpaper that was splashed with huge white flowers. John and I chose to sleep downstairs in an unfinished bedroom with a comfortable bed. We felt the need to hide away with all the emotions that had bombarded us. John shared that after he and his dad had left the hospital, they had returned to our home and removed every piece of evidence of our baby boy's precious existence. It seemed too soon, but my heart assured me that they had done this difficult task out of love for me. John would have done anything within his power to take me out of this killing pain of loss, ANYTHING! I was thankful that a few of my favorites, like his red and white checked blanket, fuzzy bunting, and ducky crib mobile had been kept. I knew I would not sleep that night, and that the only thing I wanted was to see my baby again at the funeral home, just as soon as they would allow.

When John met the funeral home staff the next morning, they agreed to honor two of my requests: that John Ryan hold a ducky from his crib mobile and that he be covered with his fuzzy yellow bunting in the little white casket that his daddy had chosen. Helen and I met at some point the next day with the priest who would preside at John Ryan's funeral service. We chose the scriptures and two songs: a special arrangement of "Bless the Beasts and the Children" from New York and "Ode to Joy". I had written a poem to our baby which his Grandma Helen agreed to read aloud. Outside of that, I just wanted to stay by my baby's side telling him over and over how much I loved him until I could no more. My precious little boy had taught me so much about courage, and John Ryan's brief presence in our lives would impact our family and its future forever. I wanted him to leave with all the love I could send. Touching his sleeping lifeless body was still so much better than never being able to touch him at all. I never wanted to leave him. Not this way.

We had decided previously not to have Elizabeth and Ondrea attend the funeral. They were only five and six years old, and having them witness so much raw pain and grief from their mom, dad and others did not seem wise. We accepted my mother's next door neighbor's gracious offer to have them stay with her for the day and make fabric Christmas decorations. The girls were thrilled at the prospect of spending time with Irene's dog Otto. After all these years, I have wondered from time to time whether this was the right decision. It is so difficult to second guess the calls of the heart.

John Ryan's funeral was as beautiful as any baby's funeral can be, with a lot of sadness and just a whisper of beauty to make it bearable. I barely remember the service, but I know many people important to us were there to offer their sympathy and support. There were no manuals to guide and lead us through the piercing grief of child loss, no magical healing words, condolences, or actions that could even come close to taming the raging fury of this grief. There is something about a mother's loss that makes the permanence of their child's death so unfathomable. I believe that it is the most brutal loss a human can bear. One of the saddest parts of grief was strikingly evident: I would have to walk every painful step alone. Grief is a solo affair. Each of us would approach our grief with different perceptions and experiences, requiring our own customized travel plans. It would be necessary to walk our tortuous journey single file through a long, narrow tunnel for one. We would each be contorted and pushed forward and into places unknown. This was difficult for John, who wanted so desperately to stay near and protect me from this hellacious process. And it was painful for me to watch him understand that he couldn't be my companion in grief. Each of us would have to travel alone. Though John Ryan's life had been brief, it felt as if we had had him for a lifetime.

Very shortly after John Ryan died, I sensed that there was a choice before me that I had to acknowledge. Did I want to rejoin life or disconnect from it forever? When a piece of me left this world, my human instinct was to follow. My heart was saying 'GO WITH HIM', but my mind was saying 'STAY HERE'. I would learn later that this is a real phenomenon which grief experts call "yearning". I could not conceive of being separated from my baby. He was completely dependent on us to take care of his medical needs. My baby needed to be comforted, rocked in warm blankets, and held next to my heart. He needed my presence around the clock, as his life literally and totally depended on it. This powerful yearning to join John Ryan thankfully began to fade away with each smile and hug from my two sweet girls. They constantly were trying their hardest to make their mommy smile again, and they were so deserving of having all of me back. They became my motivation to rejoin life. Eventually, their pull won the tug of war within me.

I often awoke at night in a sweat and panic. I felt I needed to get to the cemetery to bring my baby boy out of the ground and into the warmth of my arms. The thought of John Ryan's cold lifeless body alone and underground was more than my heart could bear. I physically felt as if my heavy heart would explode with sadness many times throughout days and nights that followed. Having never lost a child before, I was unaware that people in grief can develop Broken Heart Syndrome. It is not imagined. It is a true ailment called takotsubo cardiomyopathy, and in rare cases can cause death.

Grief has no timing, and it has its way with you when it decides to visit. I vividly remember standing over the stove fixing supper for my family when out of nowhere I dissolved into a puddle of tears. At times like this, rather than letting my family witness more sadness, I would get into the car and just drive until my thoughts and emotions were manageable again. My car knew the route by heart. With the radio blasting tunes, I would head north on Elm Street. After a couple miles, I would make a right turn and another quick right into a cul de sac...the one with the cozy two-story gray house where John Ryan's cardiologist lived. I guess it brought me some sad peace, and peace has no price that is too high in grief. On one of those crying cruises, from out of nowhere the song "Bless the Beasts and the Children" came over the radio. It shocked me. Not only was it atypical to hear this song on that radio channel, but it was the exact arrangement of the song I had special ordered from New York for John Ryan's funeral. I knew in my heart this could not be a coincidence. The return trip home was peaceful. I had found my smile again.

How I yearned to have a baby in my arms once more. Since the death of John Ryan, my arms had felt so empty, so useless, so heavy. I began to experience panic at the thought of never being able to fill them again. I had made it clear to my gynecologist not to proceed with the scheduled tubal ligation following my C-section if something did not look right with our baby. He did not honor my request. Back in 1976, the possibility of surgically reversing a tubal ligation was extremely slim. I made many calls, while in tears, to the doctor's office to see if my surgery could be reversed. I kept hoping for a different answer every time. Finally I learned that unfortunately my fallopian tubes had been severed and cauterized during surgery. Reversal was out of the question. I was again devastated. In addition to the loss of my baby, I now mourned my inability to ever bear another child. I also felt strongly betrayed by my doctor. When I realized the futility of any further attempts, I hung up and collapsed into a heap of tears on top of our bed.

Feeling the need to find someone who could connect with child loss, I reached out to a friend Esther. She and her husband Ron had lost their little girl Sarah at age six in a drowning accident. Esther was setting up a Palliative care unit at a local hospital and was an R.N. working in the area of death and dying. I sought out her help in assembling a group for bereaved parents. I also called on the expertise of a well-respected friend Dick, who ran counseling groups for parents and kids in our community. With the help of my two friends, we were able to organize a meeting of ten to twelve people, all grieving the loss of a child. Dick's approach was simple but powerful. Seated in a circle, one by one we each told our own truth and story of loss. Husbands and wives had the opportunity to tell their stories independently and without spousal input. As John spoke, I realized it was actually the first time that I had heard my husband's feelings regarding the loss of our baby. Witnessing our individual grief stories and the compassionate support from other group members was so meaningful that it pushed my grief journey ahead greatly. I now felt understood and so much less lonely in my grief. I realized how badly I needed to have my story heard, and I continued to stay open and aware for any spiritual connections I'd see or feel that were sent from my son. I craved assurance that my baby was safe and at peace.

A few years after John Ryan's death, Mother's Day was about to roll around again. Child loss gives this holiday a changed and melancholy dimension. It's as if a veil of sadness descends and shadows over a bereaved mother. One night, when John was out of town and the girls were in their rooms sound asleep, I was startled and jolted upright in bed by a distinct little voice. It rang through my ears in words with piercing clarity saying, "Hi Mommy!" With a child-like quality and an alien tonality and pitch, the words lasered through my slumber. I knew right away this sweet message was meant for me and had come from my beautiful boy. It did not frighten me, but rather spread warm peace throughout me. I fell back into my pillow with a smile on my face, knowing that John Ryan had come by just in time to say hello for Mother's Day. Spiritual messages occur randomly and always when I am least expecting it. I just know that when they do happen, without a doubt the connection is real and strengthens my inner peace.

Part Two

JEFFREY THOMAS MADDOCK

*A seed, planted with words, watered with time, and given sunlight by the
impeccable timing of fate blooms the flower of divine change.*

Judi Maddock

"Putting one foot in front of the other" described my actions perfectly in the weeks following the death of our baby. Daily demands of
a life with a husband and two children helped gently nudge me forward
reminding me that I still had purpose. John Ryan's death had not stripped
that away from me. The growth of my motivation took place in tiny
steps forward. I kept a positive face while taking my role of mothering
very seriously to reassure my girls that life would go on.

After my world had fallen apart, I realized that I had to model to my
girls that I could be strong and set goals for myself again. I decided to
pursue a certification as a learning diagnostician. I had already earned a
Bachelor of Science in Elementary Education. This added certification

would allow me to test, diagnose, and instruct children with learning differences. My university coursework was very rigorous, but I could take a couple of classes at a time, some at night. I was excited to be accepted and was committed from the start to maintaining a balance between my dual roles as student and mother. It was time for me to get out of my heart and into my head. Within the comfortable confines of my personal "Command Center" my brain could make all necessary decisions and maintain some illusion of control over my emotion. More at ease living in my mind, I hoped that my heart and emotions could rest for now.

Most nights, after putting the girls to bed, I retreated to my bathtub, allowing the solace of warm bubbly water to soothe my brain and body. Being dominantly an auditory learner, I reviewed my lecture notes aloud. If my bathroom walls could only have talked, they would have been impressive. I filled my brain with a plethora of lists to be memorized for tests, along with assessment information, diagnostic techniques, statistics, dates of pertinent court decisions, and the latest research in child brain development. My brain felt exhausted at night. Looking back now, I realize that this new academic endeavor did its job by keeping me in my head most of the time and away from my feelings. This has been my mode of survival since childhood.

Coping with grief could still be so difficult. Sadness traveled with me as my life was busy building new purpose. Even though despair still pulled me back, it somehow also pushed me ahead. It was a complicated and confusing season, but my life began to feel movement and direction once again. After obtaining my certification, I ended up interviewing with the Fargo Public Schools. As I entered the formal interview with several people sitting around a long oval table, all with questions in hand, I felt surprisingly confident. My sincere passion to work with children who had learning differences must have shone through. I left thinking that I had laid it all on the line. The next day I was offered the position. I was beyond thrilled. My self-worth had needed this for some time. My new position would be an excellent opportunity to recreate myself after loss. Little did I know then how beneficial this certification would be for me, not just as a future classroom teacher but as an adoptive parent.

John was still traveling a good share of the work week. He serviced a large tri-state territory and did a very good job of keeping us clothed, fed, and comfortable. Always my biggest encourager, John totally backed my return to education and the opportunities it might bring. He was extremely excited and proud when he learned that I had landed the job. I accepted the position feeling that it would be advantageous to us as a family, and certainly a second income would be welcomed. Other than finishing up my student teaching and then pursuing the learning disabilities certification, I had been at home with the girls. The timing seemed right. I was a product of the Fargo Public School System, and now my children were being educated within it as well. It was a highly rated school system of which I was proud to be a part. I was assigned to Longfellow Elementary in the far north reaches of Fargo. The principal was one of my former science teachers, and placement there felt like "old home week". Having the job of my dreams was exciting and made me feel so professional.

Meanwhile the desire to grow a larger family frequented our thoughts. Since college, John and I were well aware that we each adored children. One night, sitting together on the bright red and orange quilted couch in my parents' den, we explored exactly how many children we each wanted. John came from a family of nine children, and I was relieved that we both agreed on the number four. Talking further, we discussed how even more perfect it would be to have two biological children and two adopted children. Now, eleven years later, with two beautiful little girls and the loss of our precious son, we decided to act upon those words.

I made some inquiry calls to The Children's Village, a local adoption agency. The process was long. We made our way through the initial application and began our case study with a wonderful social worker named Carol. Once approved, we were advised of the long wait ahead. Could the wait be God's plan to give us more time to accept John Ryan's death? We were thrilled to be on our way to becoming parents once again. This exciting news comforted and brought our extended families happiness too, knowing that we would have another chance to add a new little miracle to our family. We were ecstatic to be officially placed on the infant male adoption list. The girls, now seven and eight, began to ask daily where this baby was.

We went about our busy lives. Not long after, we decided to expand our adoption search to include an infant boy of any mixed race. We were well aware that there was a "premium" on Caucasian babies, but we knew that we would love whatever baby God placed in our lives. As we shared our decision with friends, we were surprised at some of the comments we received. Many came from supposedly well-educated people with open minds. This was very unsettling, and it began to lead us down the road of doubt. Realizing that our geographical area and current level of community acceptance for diversity might not be fair to a mixed-race child, we decided to return to our original plan. When we told the girls, Elizabeth was particularly unhappy. Hands on hips she retorted, "You mean we're just going to get a plain old white kid?"

After three years, we still were waiting. Every day we got up and waited some more, and the girls were increasingly impatient. We tried to stay absorbed in our lives and look less at the calendar and clock. My sister Nancy's college friend gifted our family with an amazing little pair of bright yellow Oshkosh overalls. We decided to hang them in the kitchen on a baby hanger right next to our yellow wall phone. They would stay on the wall until the long-awaited phone call came. Those adorable overalls sweetened the wait and gave us a feeling of hope each time we passed them.

During those three years of waiting, our grief over losing John Ryan had become a little less raw and had started to settle into our souls, although it was always just a breath away. I was committed to bringing John Ryan forward with me. Now he was embedded in my heart, as we copiloted a new life together. He became a part of who I am. In time, all of us seemed to find reasons to smile and to enjoy life more fully once again.

At Christmas in 1979, presents for this new little boy waited under the tree with gift tags that said "Baby Joshua". Right after Christmas, I felt the need to shake things up a bit. Perhaps this baby needed a new and different name to help bring him to us sooner. The name Joshua, always a favorite of mine, was put on the back burner, and we started to consider another name choice.

I returned to school in January 1980 to find a large number of students had been referred for assessment. Faith, our speech pathologist,

34

and I assessed each student and teamed up with our school psychologist who tested intellectual ability. When learning differences were diagnosed, it was my responsibility to prepare an Individual Educational Plan for each struggling learner. That meant hours and hours of handwritten paperwork that shared observations, test results, and learning objectives for those who were admitted into our programs. Each of the triplicate carbon copies had to be filed in various places for safe keeping. It was all consuming, but I really enjoyed the challenge of pinpointing the learning problem of each child and coming up with solutions to better teach them.

One day, as I sat at my cluttered work table, a voice on the intercom asked me to come to the office for a phone call. I was half irritated at being interrupted, as I was on a productive roll. On the other end of the line was Carol, our caseworker. She said the words we were waiting to hear: "Judi, I think we have a baby boy for you!" With a pounding heart, I grabbed a piece of scratch paper and began writing down every word of her description. I still have this paper today, to remind me of the incredible elation and excitement I felt at being told that this "long pregnancy" was finally over. Our baby was here. I must have asked her a million questions about our little boy's health, the birth mother's prenatal care, how much he weighed, his Apgar scores at birth, and everything else fluttering through my mind. He was a healthy four-week-old infant, and we could pick him up the very next day.

I was out the door in a flash. I had told the girls that they would be the first to hear the news, and that I would show up at their school to surprise them. Back then you could walk in and out of elementary schools without having to check in at the main office. My heart was thumping as I galloped up the long granite stairway and knocked on the big oak classroom door of Mr. Peterson's room. Elizabeth's face turned bright red as she raced to the door to see why I was there. She guessed right away! After announcing to her class that her baby brother was finally here, Elizabeth grabbed her things, and we raced to Ondrea's second grade classroom. She, too, bubbled with excitement as we flew down the steps and out of the school. Even though home was only two short blocks away, we couldn't get to the yellow wall phone fast enough. It just didn't seem real. The overalls could come down from the wall at last.

John, finishing up a week of travel in Sioux Falls, SD, had just returned to his hotel room for a nap. When he picked up the phone, I told him, "You're not going to believe this, but the adoption agency called, and we have a baby boy!" He was beyond happy and immediately made plans to travel home. The girls and I gobbled down a quick supper and talked about what we needed to get for the big day. We drove to a store called Children's Palace for some "coming home" clothes for our baby. We chose a little blue onesie and a baby blue knit hooded sweater that zipped up the back. I'm sure we packed a few more items into the shopping cart as well. We had kept John Ryan's red-checked blanket. It was bittersweet to be using it again, but it seemed right. Our little one's crib was all set up and thankfully everything was pretty much ready for his homecoming. Once the girls were in bed, I tried to calm myself as I waited for John's headlights to shine through the front window. Staying up late meant fewer hours until we could meet this long-awaited child. It was hard for me to sleep that night. I felt like a child experiencing a thousand Christmas Eves rolled into one. John, tired from his long trip home, had no problems drifting off.

On a blustery February 20ᵗ, 1980, we loaded into the car. I remember exactly what I wore under my rabbit fur jacket: a gray wool blazer and matching wool pants. I felt like I needed to dress up a bit for this exciting occasion. John wore his camel top coat as well as a huge smile of anticipation. When we entered the adoption agency, the receptionist greeted us, and we were ushered into a small room with two matching couches. At that time in the world of adoption, everything was kept highly secretive and strictly confidential. Arrival times were staggered to protect the identity of the foster mother who would deliver our baby to the agency that morning. We were confined to this small space to nervously await our child. Finally, there was a long-awaited rap on our door, and in came our friend Sue, a social worker at the agency. In her arms she held our precious bundle of new hope.

I stood up and reached out my arms to cradle him to my chest. He felt so warm and healthy, like a baby should feel. It was a really healing moment for our family and certainly for me as a mom. The girls and John huddled around to touch him and sneak a peek. I eventually laid him down on a blanket so everyone could see him better. He was so beautiful and perfect in every way. His chiseled little face wore a serious look. He reminded me of a little Irishman. Peering into those little eyes I thought, "Oh my God, I have so much love to give to you. You have no idea what happiness and hope you have returned to our lives in just the last few minutes." We changed him into his "going home" clothes and wrapped him in the yellow fuzzy bunting and the red-checked blanket. I snuggled him in close all the way to our waiting car. I never wanted to let him go of him. I breathed in his beautiful baby scent as we left the parking lot.

We went straight to my mom's house in Moorhead, hoping to surprise her, but they were not home. We continued on back to Fargo, and as we were passing the Moorhead post office we spotted my mom, stepdad Morris and brother Steve walking to their parked car. This could not be more coincidental! We slowly turned the car around the corner. I was holding our baby in the front seat. In those days there was no such thing as a safe car seat. I wound the car window down just enough for them to see the baby. My mom began yelling with excitement. We told them to meet us at John's mom and dad's home in Fargo, where Grandma Helen, Grandpa Bernie, and Aunt Sheila greeted us. As Jeffrey was passed from one person to the next, I could sense that our baby boy wasn't a big fan of all the commotion and new faces. Once we got him changed and fed and snuggled to sleep, he seemed happier. We were anxious to get him home and settled into his new surroundings. This was the house where John Ryan had died four years earlier. Now, bringing another baby through that door, we were making new and happier memories. It was an unforgettable and blessed event.

We didn't yet have a name for our child, since we had decided to opt for a different one just weeks before. For the next few days, I was on the phone often with my mom trying to decide on one we all liked. Nothing really hit me, until one day she said, "What about Jeffrey?" That name just sounded right. Everyone else agreed. Shortly thereafter, we chose my sister Nancy and John's brother Tom to be godparents. That led to a full name: Jeffrey Thomas Maddock. Our baby had a name. All was right with the world. I can't even put into words how much joy and how much love that little squirt brought into our lives. He was the love of his sisters' lives and ours from the moment we met him.

Every child is a gift, but adoption means that someone else is entrusting you with the chance to raise the child that they brought into this world. Adoption carries so many feelings of duty and responsibility. I immediately felt an obligation to do right by Jeffrey's birth mother. I only hope that at some point in her life, she has come to understand what a profound and immeasurable gift of love and change that she gave our family through this beautiful baby boy. I swear that our lungs were exhaling pure joy.

I wanted so desperately to stay home and take care of Jeffrey myself. Unfortunately, I had only a matter of days to find a placement in home daycare for him. In 1980, Fargo teacher contracts had no provision for adoption leave. With only three months left in the school year, it was necessary to convince myself that I could do what countless other working moms did: find a loving daycare for my baby. The girls already were occasional participants in an after-school daycare near the school. Finding a home daycare that would take an infant would be a little more difficult. Fortunately, I found Darlene, a kind, soft-spoken lady who lived not far from us. I felt that she would provide gentle, quality care and that Jeffrey would be safe with this experienced mother in a loving home. My angst was somewhat relieved.

Each morning, I would deliver the girls to school and then wind my way to Darlene's house to drop off Jeffrey. That first few days, I cried all the way from daycare to school. I would tell myself that every other working mom had to be feeling the same way and that they seemed to manage. I would just have to make it up to him as soon as I got him in my arms again. During my first three years as a learning disabilities teacher, I was figuring out how to balance being a working mom with my commitment to children at school. I felt so blessed to love my work. The responsibilities of my new career took me to places that completely absorbed my mind and allowed me to not constantly think about my baby for several hours. I tried to use my time efficiently so I could get out the door at 3:30, as I had my baby to pick up and the girls to see. My number one job was to not be behind school doors any longer than necessary.

I operated more or less as a single mom. John continued to work four days on the road, coming home on Thursdays. Each day, I would race home to anxiously collect my little brood. As soon as we got settled in, my focus turned completely toward Jeffrey. The girls were more than happy running around the neighborhood playing with friends. This precious time with Jeffrey let me bond with this baby that had taken up residency in my heart and life.

I noticed very early on that Jeffrey was really into moving and he was good at it. His vision was very keen, and his eye-hand coordination was impressive. However, he did not like to sleep at night, in part because as soon as I heard a little noise that was even remotely atypical, I ran into his room to make sure he was alright. My hypervigilance was likely due to having lost John Ryan in his sleep.

Jeffrey's room was only about ten feet from ours. Very active and impressively coordinated, he began standing up in his crib at the age of five months. Often, he would wake up and jabber loudly to himself. I would lie there listening to my healthy babbling baby while counting my blessings. Eventually the fussiness would start, and my feet would hit the floor. I was by his crib in an instant to feed, rock, and lull him back to sleep. Needless to say, the quality of my sleep was suffering greatly.

One night, I was jarred awake by a sound emanating from Jeffrey's room—one I had never heard before. From the back of his throat came the strangest guttural sounds, somewhere between a diesel truck left idling and the growl of a wounded animal. Racing into his room in a huge adrenaline rush, I found my baby standing up in his crib. He was batting and knocking off most of the yellow duckies on his crib mobile. He seemed to be as happy as a clam entertaining himself. My girls had never made these sounds! Influenced by the whole Marlo Thomas "Free to be you and me" era, my plan had been to treat him just as I had treated my girls. I was going to resist conditioning my child into sexual stereotyping of any kind and to give him the freedom to develop as he was meant to be. Well, that night I began to consider the possibility that there could indeed be inherent differences between raising a little boy and raising a little girl.

This exhausting pattern of broken sleep continued on for nearly three and a half years. Getting up and settling him back down a few times each night made me realize that Jeffrey had me trained. No matter how many times I was resolved to let him cry it out, I just couldn't stand the panic I felt inside. I probably created a good share of the problem myself. I think I was actually dealing with trauma, because I was a mother who had already lost a baby in his sleep. I was so blasted tired that one day I just had to lie down for a minute or so between students. I rolled my big yellow window shade down, locked the door, and found a corner out of sight where I could rest on the floor. I kept thinking that it could be the end of me and this job that I loved so much if anyone came in and found me. I was extremely desperate, but it was the first and last time I ever shut my eyes on the job.

Jeffrey continued to be early with everything motor. He stood up around furniture at six months and walked at eight months. It was comical to see this infant boy walking through the house as if he had been walking forever. We realized that we had been blessed with a healthy and strong child—and we never took that for granted. When he turned one, he started turning his foot inward. The doctor recommended that his foot be placed in a cast for a short time to try to correct the turn. The cast did not slow Jeffrey down one bit as he clomped around the house at breakneck speed. He was drawn to objects that were small and intricate, and proved to be unusually dexterous for his age. Our little boy also began to reveal unique quirks. He was a picky eater, and survived mostly on yogurt, bananas, orange juice, and oatmeal. His sensitivity to the feeling of certain textures of food and clothing was evident as the months went by. As a toddler, the very first thing he wanted to do when he got home from daycare was to take off his clothes and get into his soft tan football pajamas with no tag. Home was a place where he could turn off the world, and the pajamas made it perfectly clear that he was going nowhere. He was a ball of beautiful energy.

Jeffrey's first little friend was a boy named Phillip who lived right across the street. I heard Phillip before I ever actually saw him. He was a cute little blondie with a vocal presence that would knock your socks off. Jeffrey met little Kevin on a Hot Wheel spin around the block. Before long these three were like a little Harley gang. They rode at top speed, screeching at the top of their lungs. There was nothing but pure joy on their little faces. Kevin and Jeffrey attempted to match the volume and pitch of Phillip's screeching voice while speeding up and down the sidewalk. Working with a speech pathologist, I had become aware of a thing called vocal nodules. I was concerned, but try to explain that to a three-year-old. I had to choose my battles, and I couldn't win this one. For better or worse, I was continually hypervigilant with this poor child. I allowed him quite a bit of freedom, too, because I didn't want to completely squelch his independent streak. He needed to be physical and outside enjoying his friends. Since I didn't know how much of that energy he was able to get rid of at daycare, I decided to make moving around and going from activity to activity a priority when he was home.

Jeffrey also changed daycares a few times, because I was constantly reevaluating whether I had found the right one for him. Change was not easy for Jeffrey. I recognized that it took extra patience and understanding to really read and understand him, so I was searching for someone who "got him". Without knowing it, I was well on my way to becoming the major interpreter for my child in this world. I easily slid into this role without even being aware of it. I wanted the world to show him acceptance and understanding, and so I attempted to become Jeffrey's bridge to the world.

When Jeffrey was three, we thought it would be good for him to go to preschool a couple of days a week. My good friend's daughter Megan went to a daycare lady named Karen and was enrolled in a nearby preschool. I thought hanging around his friend Megan would provide Jeffrey a good transition into preschool. Karen was a sweet and sensitive lady, and she agreed to take Jeffrey in. It went great, except that during their more structured times, they all had to sing about Jesus. This was not the best part of daycare in Jeffrey's eyes. Our house always had music, but we had always played classical music to put our kids to sleep at night. As years went by, Jeffrey referred to classical music as the "good music". Interestingly, this "good music" contained no words.

When Jeffrey attended preschool, I continued to notice more interesting quirks. Jeffrey wasn't so sure about this whole confinement thing and following so many directions. He and his teacher Connie shared a secret signal to help him remember to get back on track. He wasn't naughty but he just seemed hesitant to join in and conform totally. At the preschool programs, it was obvious he didn't like performing in front of people. Not easily remembering words to songs certainly did not help, so it was easier to not perform or to act silly. This was a small red flag, but preschool was good for him in many ways. Jeffrey never did enjoy singing. Years down the road, we would learn that Jeffrey had an actual deficit in auditory processing and auditory memory. With that information, Jeffrey's early quirks around singing and following verbal directions made total sense. My role as Jeffrey's personal interpreter and its reasons were not imagined after all.

Our realtor friend Steve (or Uncle Steve as he called himself) decided that he would help us look for a different house. Part of the reason I had originally wanted to buy my childhood home was to erase some of the trauma I grew up with there and to fill it with happier memories. Living there turned out to be both semi-healing and semi-unsettling. Certainly, losing a child in that house haunted me, and after eight years it was time to pass it on to somebody else who could fill it with fresh happy karma.

We were looking to upsize a bit and be closer to the school where I worked. Steve showed us two to three houses in the area. One I fell in love with. It stood directly across the street from the "homey gray two-story house" that I had walked and driven by countless times—the home of John Ryan's pediatric cardiologist. Uncle Steve did some financial magic and we bought the house.

Fortunately, our old house sold in about a week's time. The new house had already been vacated, so we had permission to put our belongings in the house even though we had technically not closed yet. The night before closing, we drove our cars into the garage early in the day and accidentally on purpose forgot to leave. We were sneaking around the house avoiding the windows and not turning on any lights. Early the next morning, we got up early to drop our girls off at school and Jeffrey at daycare before arriving at the mortgage agency for our official closing. Finally, that night, we would light up our new beautiful home with no guilt. Life was good.

The girls were already in junior high school and less excited than we were about leaving the old neighborhood. They had loved the diversity that they had left behind and did not appreciate moving into this more affluent area where the kids seemed to be more "cookie cutter" in nature. Most came from homogeneous circumstances and professional family incomes. A good share of these children had traveled the world and lacked for nothing, or so my girls thought. In time, their overgeneralization proved to be incorrect. They made lifelong friends and we shared a wonderful life together as a family in this house. Jeffrey had also suffered the loss of his little Hot Wheels gang. There were no visible small children in the new neighborhood, and I became Jeffrey's playmate. We bought him every piece of sports equipment he desired, but what he really wanted was someone his age to play with. I recall one afternoon looking out into our big backyard through the kitchen window and bursting into tears. I wondered what we had done. I felt so guilty about our move when I looked at this lonely little four-year-old with no one to play with but Mom.

A few months later a rash of little boys popped up, seemingly out of nowhere. Soon a new little gaggle of boys joined Jeffrey in the grass circle in the middle of our cul-de-sac. Each day after school and throughout the summer, this became a Mini-Olympics zone. Jeffrey was one happy ringleader, organizing the play as they moved seamlessly from one sport to the next. Just about every conceivable type of sports equipment was scattered about this neighborhood playground. This went on for most of their elementary years, and my heart was full and grateful for the many hours of play that circle of grass provided to this once-lonely little boy and his friends.

Jeffrey joined me as a kindergartner at Longfellow School. I was more than a little leery about his initiation into formal education. I was happy that he would see some familiar neighborhood faces. I was determined to expect the best, knowing he was in good hands.

My resource room was tucked away in a far corner of the school. We had no telephones in our rooms and communicated with the office via an intercom system. My position required physical access to phones and the office in order to schedule student/parent IEP meetings and access student files. I easily put on miles of walking every day down the long hallway to the office. One day as I rounded the corner, I glanced through the large glass windows in the office and saw my son sitting outside the principal's office. Something was up. I entered the office, and my eyes zeroed in on Jeffrey. Indeed, he had been sent in by the music teacher. I recall thinking that if this was how kindergarten was starting, Longfellow School was going to be a long stretch. After questioning him, he shared that upon his hesitation to join in on a non-traditional method of

43

singing music called Kodaly he was asked to make a choice: stay and participate in Kodaly, which involved the use of hand signs to sight-read music and learn and use pitch in singing, or go to the office. It was a no brainer. My black-and-white child quickly chose the office. If he didn't enjoy music before, he wouldn't flourish in the Kodaly program. I was horrified, but understood how this type of music training was way too illogical and out there for him. I let him work this one out with the teacher and principal.

The classroom was not going well either. His teacher was not willing to go outside of her comfort zone to accommodate his weakness in auditory processing, which had not yet been formally diagnosed. Socially, he found it very difficult to read body language, and he was quickly convinced he was never going to be understood or liked by this teacher. I knew in my gut that this train had to be turned around quickly for the sake of Jeffrey, and his teacher. It was just not a fit, and I pleaded to have him changed into a different kindergarten room. This was a bit awkward professionally, but it worked out satisfactorily all the way around. Jeffrey ended his year on a much better note with a different teaching approach. His first-grade teacher took a liking to Jeffrey, and he fit better in a more structured environment where he felt accepted and where things were very predictable.

Part Three

JOSHUA NEIL MADDOCK

I always get where I'm going by walking away from where I've been.

Winnie the Pooh

When Jeffrey was preschool age, we decided to adopt again. We wanted to give Jeffrey a sibling to grow up around, and we believed we had enough love to bring another child into our fold. We went through all the necessary procedures and paperwork, had our case study completed, and were approved to adopt a male child over the age of three, which put this adoption into the category of "special needs". By this time, the girls were aware that this process would most likely involve another long wait. Secretly, because we weren't adopting an infant, I hoped our wait might be shorter. Life continued to roll down a busy and relatively smooth road, as once again we played the adoption waiting game.

Still I was caught off guard on a cloudy fall day in 1986, when Sharon, our caseworker, called me at school to say that my "four-year pregnancy" was over. With butterflies in my stomach, sitting at the same desk in the same office where I had learned about Jeffrey's arrival, I grabbed a yellow legal pad and began scribbling copious notes about a five-year-old named Joshua. Hearing his name, I knew this was the child meant for us. I was so grateful that we had made the impulsive decision to change our original name choice for Jeffrey, because it would have been uncanny and confusing to have two sons named Joshua. This was the "real" Joshua, who would hopefully join our lives forever. Unfortunately, he had come from a complicated and messed-up family of origin that had included drug and alcohol abuse, emotional and physical abuse, and neglect. He had already been in three different foster homes, and a recent placement had fallen through. The adoption agency needed to be extremely cautious and was very protective this time around in finding the right family for this fragile child.

While John and I were excited, the other children were a bit more reserved and tentative about the prospect of a new brother. Jeffrey had difficulty with quick change and the element of surprise, and another daughter thought maybe we should slow this train down, as our family of five felt perfectly fine to her. However, the next weekend John and I met Joshua in a town nearly 300 miles from Fargo. We understood that Joshua's heart was fragile from the rejection and trauma he had already experienced. Moving forward with commitment, we decided that our visit meant this child would become ours, sight unseen. We would take him home and into our hearts and love him forever.

All we knew for sure was that he had brown eyes and was bright and curious, yet I felt calmed by the certainty of what felt like God's plan for us. We were committed to filling in his craters of hurt with enough love to make the possibility of a wonderful life and future within his reach. This little warrior had been through more abandonment and maltreatment in his first five years than most adults would experience in a lifetime. We arrived late morning at the adoption agency, our hearts thumping wildly as sat in the lobby.

After what seemed like forever, I peeked around the corner and down the bare hallway. Suddenly, I glimpsed a little boy with longish dark hair dash across the hallway like a moving target of bright blue. "John! I think I just saw him!" I whispered loudly. I clutched John's arm and braced myself. A few minutes later, I sensed someone standing beside me. In a moment I was peering into Joshua's beautiful brown eyes, which were nervously darting around the room. All he needed to say was "Hello" in his cute little voice, and I fell in love. In his chocolate eyes, I saw trepidation and the light of hope shining simultaneously. He had a finely sculptured face that I found adorable. His light brown glasses were anchored tightly to his head by a band, and he had the cutest mouth full of tiny, white baby teeth. Joshua's feet were jammed into a pair of outgrown and overly worn cowboy boots. He would be ours, and I could hardly wait to mother him. With a bright aura surrounding him, he had very easily stolen our hearts.

We left the adoption agency with Joshua in hand and headed to McDonald's. As Joshua twirled around and around on his stool, John and I attempted to break the ice with a little light conversation. I felt myself growing dizzier by the minute with each twirl of the chair, and finally it seemed a good time to head out to our next venue, the zoo. Before we left McDonalds, Joshua carefully wrapped up the small amount of his leftover food and tucked it into the pocket of his jacket. When we reached the zoo, Joshua's eyes glazed with excitement as he danced through the animal exhibits. He allowed me to carry him in my arms to give his boots a rest from time to time, and we took adorable pictures to remember this special day.

Two hours flew by quickly and soon it was time to head back to the agency. As I turned around to face him buckled into the back seat, his eyes revealed a troubling message. They seemed to be saying that although this was fun, he would never see us again. I felt the need to reassure him, so I promised that we were coming back the following weekend. Unfortunately, in Joshua's experience, all promises were made to be broken. This time, I was praying that he would take the risk to believe mine. With Joshua safely returned, we got back into our car. John and I took what seemed like a perfectly synchronized deep breath. We'd experienced so much energy and light in this little boy and were clueless as to where saying yes to all of it would lead us. We were committed to embracing the journey.

We made a few more visits, including one with the entire family. We hoped that Elizabeth, Ondrea, and Jeffrey would see the depth of our commitment to Joshua. In the hotel, the kids had fun playing in the pool and seemed to mesh together well. We began wondering how many more visits it would take to make the agency realize that we were serious and ready to bring him into our family and home forever. There would be no backing out on our part. Also, driving 600-plus miles every weekend to see him was really putting a strain on our family and Joshua. I pushed the agency to complete the adoption process sooner rather than later. They agreed, and plans were made for a final visit to hold his "Forever Home" placement ceremony. Only Jeffrey was able to accompany us, as the girls had school commitments.

The touching candle lighting ceremony to celebrate Joshua's life and journey from his birth home, to his foster homes, and now to his forever family included his foster parents, case workers, and us. Joshua and his brother Jeffrey bonded while maneuvering toy race cars in an imaginary racetrack around our feet. As we gathered around a large conference table, nervous chatter and mixed emotions flooded the room. Many present had attempted to protect and shelter the heart of Joshua. Eventually, the boys were asked to join us at the table, and the service began. I'm quite sure Jeffrey and Joshua's favorite part was the cake and ice cream that followed. With tearful hugs from his foster family, we headed to our car. We had left home with one little boy, and were returning with two. Leaving the only place and people he had ever known was hard for Joshua. It broke my heart to see tears rolling down his face. I can't imagine what was going through his mind as we drove away. All I knew is that I was both amazed and saddened at his resiliency.

When we finally pulled into our driveway, Joshua's eyes lit up. From the backseat he yelled, "Wow, Mom! It's just like Disneyland!" Our house was no match for Disneyland, yet more than Joshua could have hoped for. Our family felt complete at last. Our pact to have two biological children and adopt two children had come to fruition. Fate had now fully revealed its story.....or had it?

Busily, he set about getting acquainted with his new bedroom and his new roommate and brother. Everything had been made ready to welcome Joshua home. Bunkbeds were now side-by-side twin beds with red plaid flannel comforters and matching shams. Because Joshua had never had a room he could claim as his, I put thought into filling it with items that included both touches of Joshua and Jeffrey.

Sadly, Joshua had only one small paper bag containing a stuffed toy, his blue nylon jacket, a quilt he and his foster mom Sandy had made, a few of his plastic army men, and his pair of outgrown cowboy boots. We had already bought him new shoes, but we knew the attachment he had to his boots, which would now occupy a special spot in the double closet he shared with Jeffrey. It had been a long day, and we wanted to make his first night as routine and calm as possible. We said our goodnights and left their bedroom door and ours open in case Joshua needed us.

Joshua got in and out of bed a few times for water. Later, he was in the bathroom for an unusually long time. Heading down the short stairway to check on him, I could hear him vomiting. He flushed the toilet and tiptoed back across the hall and into bed without noticing me. I went into his room to tuck him back in bed and reassure him.

Of course he was overwhelmed by all the changes he had experienced in just this first day—but how sad to see this little boy, so used to taking care of himself, now relying on himself once again. The idea of any five-year-old paddling into the bathroom, vomiting and then putting himself back to bed without asking for help was unimaginable to me. I desperately wanted to lift the role of caregiver off his shoulders. I prayed that soon he would trust me enough to allow me to mother him.

Our years with Joshua taught me more about life than all my education, fancy certifications, and degrees ever had. Joshua had a richness of character from surviving many difficult and dangerous challenges. He was highly intelligent and became our own little version of Curious George. His precocious curiosity and impulsivity steered him from one endeavor to the next as he learned about positive and negative choices and their consequences. These were necessary and critically important lessons. Watching him try to establish and respect boundaries was difficult. He had come into our lives quite ragged around the edges. His too-small boots, banded glasses, and cute little lisp were things we could fix. The following years revealed that after so much damage, parts of this innocent young soul could never fully be mended. We would painfully discover that no amount of love, encouragement, counseling, expectation, or consistency could heal all the deep wounds and damaging hurts of his past.

Managing his own nausea was the first of many reminders of the neglect he had suffered with no adult to count on. We were thankful to have Joshua safely in our lives and wanted so badly to assure him that he was lovable and worthy of a normal and loving family and a fulfilling life. We had to break through his dense wall of distrust to allow him to trust that our love and presence would always be there for him. I knew it was going to take time, strong dedication, and a lot of patience on the part of everyone in our household—but I couldn't know just how intense and prolonged this devoted effort would be.

The agency told us that there would be a honeymoon period in which Joshua would be on his best behavior. He needed some time to acclimate and feel safe in his new environment before revealing not only his sunlight but his shadows.

Joshua started kindergarten at Longfellow School the day after Thanksgiving in 1986. He was a bright little guy who eagerly welcomed the challenges of new people and a new school. He was social and entertaining to be around, and school started off well. He began feeling more comfortable about showing us parts of his personality that we hadn't yet seen.

Just before we brought Joshua home for good, a child psychologist who completed one session of play therapy with him told us to treat him like we would any normal child, and that Joshua would be "fine". His lame comments left me incredulous. Having worked with many children, I knew plenty about the impact of those early years of development on a child. As the agency shared more details regarding the extent of abuse in Joshua's birth home and as things began to settle down some at home, I arranged individual therapy for Joshua. I wanted an outside professional to help him work through the heavy issues that stemmed from his birth home and pre-adoption years. He was matched with a younger free-spirited, high-energy woman who shared a real connection with our son in his weekly appointments. She soon agreed with me that the severity of the issues that our son faced could not be downplayed. Joshua was a little boy with some significantly deep wounds and experiences that would need to be addressed for him to resolve his past. Treating Joshua like a "normal" child was not going to be enough.

I felt like God had put this amazing social worker in Joshua's path. He loved going to see her. During their weekly sessions, she explored a lot of his early experiences in order to focus therapy goals for Joshua's mental health. As she skillfully unwrapped his past with him, she helped us realize that there were painful things about Joshua's early life that we had yet to learn. She suggested taking him to the local rape and abuse crisis center in order to explore the possibility of sexual abuse. Joshua had been neglected and rejected by those who were supposed to love him. At the very least, some boundaries had been inappropriately crossed. We knew for a fact that his birth father abused weed and alcohol and frequently held parties in their trailer after his birth mother had left for work in the evenings.

On one such night Joshua, displaying his typical curiosity, had bounded out to the living room to check out what was going on. One of the partiers convinced Joshua to pick up a cable prong and stick it into the electrical outlet. Being impulsive, he decided to try it, and suffered electrical shock and third degree burns on his arm. Joshua was made to wait until his birth mother returned home at midnight to take him to the hospital for medical attention. I can't imagine the pain and fear that this three year old must have felt as he suffered. He was hospitalized for four days, and red flags were raised by Child Protection.

At some point after this incident, the birth father and mother were divorced and the boys remained in full custody of their birth mother. They were living in a rundown trailer with no window screens or bed sheets. Food and money were scarce. Three children under the age of five were left alone unsupervised, sometimes for days. Joshua took charge of figuring out how to feed his older and younger brother by opening cans of beans and whatever might be found so they wouldn't go hungry. (To the day we lost him, he refused to eat beans!) One day, the birth mother returned home to find Joshua outside throwing the last six eggs from the refrigerator onto the sidewalk. Because the eggs were their entire food supply for the week, this was a traumatic event. Not long after, the birth mother decided she needed to give Joshua up for adoption. He was the first to go, followed shortly by the other two. After reading this in his final adoption report and coming home to this innocent little boy who had endured repeated neglect and rejection by those who were supposed to love him, I could feel my heart crack into pieces just like those eggs Joshua threw on the sidewalk.

Interestingly, several months before we ever knew about Joshua, one of my siblings told me of my own father's problem with alcoholism. This took me by surprise, as I had so rarely seen my father drink any type of alcohol. I was very curious about this new truth and began reading a library of information about codependency, alcoholism, and its effects on the children who had survived it. I sought group counseling sessions with other adult children of alcoholics and individual counseling to try to understand how to spot codependency life patterns in myself and others. Maybe this illness called alcoholism was actually behind the behavior of the father I thought was so violent and cold, and who stirred up so much trauma and chaos in our family home. Maybe he wasn't the evil man I thought he was, and his coldness and violence stemmed from a disease, not his soul.

What I saw firsthand at the age of seven was the physical and verbal abuse inflicted on my mother for years. From the time I was young, I was hypervigilant whenever my mother and father were under the same roof. I became an expert at reading their tone and kept myself on constant alert. I had to be ready to jump in between my mom and dad at all hours of the day, and especially at night. I found the strength and the courage I didn't know a little girl could have in order to protect my mom. Though small in stature, I was able to transform into a physical barrier in the middle in order to de-escalate the violence. There was no way to predict these outbreaks or what would set my dad off. Each time they frightened me to the core.

My dad was a strong man, and I realize now that my mother's life and mine were often in real danger. Once I found myself between my mother and my father as he wielded a kitchen knife. Only when dad was on the road during the week could I take off my heavy "protector's cape" for a few days. I felt safe only when he wasn't home. As I got older, he attempted to make me a victim of his rage, but I constantly was aware of my environment and all the exits. I was too quick for him and knew how to get away. Eventually, chronic emphysema meant he couldn't chase me or any of my siblings down. Unfortunately, what he couldn't do to me with his hands, he did with his words. I was verbally and emotionally abused by him as I entered my teen years. I tried to make sure we didn't share much space in order to avoid his comments.

In order to survive, I created a network of girlfriends who unknowingly allowed me frequent escapes with weekend sleepovers. This also proved to be a way to gauge normalcy in families. It wasn't difficult to see that mine was dysfunctional, and I kept the shame of that buried inside for many years. I learned to hide my home life and to preserve the white picket fence image of my cozy-looking house, never sharing what went on inside. No one knew, and I was blessed that my friends could give me the reprieve I needed from the chaos that enveloped me at home. Those friends helped construct the foundation of who I am today. I am forever grateful that 60 years later I am still blessed by their continued support. Once I learned of my dad's own difficult upbringing, I was able to form a more empathetic understanding and healing forgiveness for him. He did have feelings, and he did love me to the best of his ability. I was confused as to how kindly he treated his mother while showing little respect for mine.

Now all these years later, I felt I could use my childhood experience living with violence in a positive way to parent our new son. I knew some of what he was feeling because I had felt it too. Our similar stories bonded me tightly to him and made me all the more determined to save him from what would likely be a rocky road. This beautiful brown-eyed boy of five and his new mother would travel this twisty road of healing together, side by side. But while my added awareness of addiction helped me understand Joshua's struggles, recognizing some of these same deep issues in myself ripped me open. I would never have had the energy to deal with myself first, only to go back to repeat the process with Joshua. Now, in some ways, our healing journey would become one.

Daily, we saw evidence that Joshua's sense of trust had been completely shattered by his early life. Why should he have any reason to trust, when every adult in his life thus far had let him down and left him feeling vulnerable and unprotected? Joshua's very basic needs for security and safety had never been met. He knew no boundaries and was afraid of nothing. On the outside he was free with his affection, and he used his wit and sense of humor to charm us into believing that he was attaching. Joshua probably felt our love, but he couldn't trust it enough to allow himself to believe the love. We tried to show him in countless ways that we really did care and that we would never abandon him again. He never totally believed that. His abandonment fears were too deeply embedded, and seeing that continually ripped us apart. We poured on the love anyway, and hoped that eventually he would open his heart to it.

Jeffrey and Joshua were only 15 months apart. Their journeys were intertwined in the beginning and they had a lot of "working things out" to do as new brothers. They were like night and day. Jeffrey liked his space and liked things the way he wanted them. He had never really had to share, and now he had this little knicker knocker of a shadow following him around, playing with all his toys, and definitely invading his space. Jeffrey had tight and rigid boundaries and liked structure and predictability. Joshua was impulsive, unpredictable, and had few if any boundaries. Joshua enjoyed using his quick wit and teasing sense of humor on Jeffrey, who had a unique and very opposite way of interpreting and enjoying humor. Because Joshua was difficult for Jeffrey to trust or read, he found Joshua amusing only at a distance. The boys were polar opposites. Watching them, it was easy to anticipate the bumps that lay in the road ahead.

The two newest loves of our lives could not have been more different. As a parent, I felt challenged at all turns. I wanted to be the best mom they "never" had. My heart was so invested in doing all that was humanly possible to assure that result. Had I taken on more than I could chew? Probably, but I poured every part of me into positively raising my two beautiful boys. Parenting became extra complex and difficult due to their extremely different personalities. Trying hard to encourage and nurture the true essence of each of them, I became like a gardener. I was constantly having to decide which behaviors to save and which to discard to make room for new healthy growth and stronger blooms. The differences between them couldn't have been more apparent. One freely displayed the good, bad, and ugly of emotions; the other lacked the ability to interpret his emotions and rarely let them show.

One functioned best in the certainty of a black-and-white world with no surprises; the other flourished in a gray world open to interpretation and the chaos of change.

One didn't know how to determine where safety stopped and danger began and wore lots of band aids; the other could stop his momentum with impeccable timing to avoid disaster.

One sought to run toward the furthest edges of life; the other preferred to cling to the safety zone in the middle.

One had hygiene so impeccable we had to time his showers; the other needed to be reminded to get into the shower and stay there long enough to get wet.

One was a little Houdini who loved crawling under the pews in church and had to be dragged back by his ankles; the other sat still and with minimal movement, as rigid as a piece of steel.

One loved rules and relied on the assurance of equality and fairness; the other didn't appreciate the confinement and control of rules and preferred to make his own.

One could look right at you and lie through his little baby teeth; the other emulated Abe Lincoln by living reliably in truth.

One was full of belly laughs and spontaneous humor; the other kept humor on the back burner and rarely showed extremes of emotions.

One was naturally athletic and moved with swiftness and grace; the other found it difficult to walk and chew bubble gum at the same time.

One made friends easily and the collection grew daily; the other had a hard time becoming vulnerable enough to trust friendship outside home and neighborhood.

While one needed to be repeatedly pushed outside his comfort zone, the other needed to be constantly reined back in. One could say that my whole parenting experience was a real-life version of Tug of War, and on many days I wanted to let go of the rope.

We were still working out a few quirks with Jeffrey, especially in the areas of social skills and learning. Thankfully, his natural athletic ability would serve to push social participation and the building of friendships. Jeffrey liked the predictability of rules and lived comfortably within a black and white world. Joshua had learned out of necessity to shift his world around outside of the lines for his very survival. He thrived on creating abundant chaos and preferred living with no boundaries. Though close in age, our boys would require very different types of parenting techniques.

Joshua became exceedingly difficult to parent as time went on. Fearless, with no personal boundaries, he thwarted every attempt I made to make him feel more secure within a few guidelines. He was used to relying on his own, and acting out in negative behaviors to get the negative response he was used to getting. Living in chaos was what he knew and where he could feel a sense of his own control.

Even after months, Joshua didn't dare to be loved. I had to assume the role of disciplinarian because John's job took him on the road three to four days every week. It was exhausting. When John would return home, he could be the "good parent" and the "nice person". Joshua was a master at triangulation, and acted schmoozy and affectionate with John, leaving me to feel like the "bad parent" and the "mean person" because I set boundaries I had mothered two children and worked with hundreds of others—but nothing seemed to be working. I had already tried every trick I could conceive of with no consistent success. I felt frustrated and not at all like the good mother I thought I was. This was a personal disappointment after all my teaching and parenting years. Until Joshua arrived, I thought I had this parenting thing in the bag.

John and I looked forward to the day that we wouldn't have to walk on eggshells for fear of triggering Joshua to act out his hurt. We had already learned how to guide him through many downward spirals. Each time we were relieved and amazed by the way he could rebound. We had to love and accept him with all these frailties, even when he tried his hardest to prove to us his belief that he was unlovable at the core. Every single day with Joshua was a test, and we were part of his experiment. He seemed determined to break us, and we were just as determined that he wouldn't. For years, and with persistence, Joshua pushed me out to the end of the tree branch with his endless challenging behaviors. Each time, he was sure he could force us into a state of surrender. But we were committed to turning this trajectory around. John and I were in this together and hoped that Joshua would eventually be able to feel our love and believe it. Joshua would never experience us giving up on him. From the start, there was an eternal joy and goodness of heart inside our Joshua that couldn't be destroyed no matter how hard he tried to convince us. He showed undying resilience each time we reeled him back in off the branch.

Early on, I had taken Joshua for vision and hearing checks. He had already gone through three sets of ear tubes and would have five by the age of seven. Shopping for new glasses, with no bands, we settled on a pair that I adored on him. They were a deep chocolate brown and accentuated his eyes perfectly. We became frequent customers at the optical shop, bringing in bent or broken glasses once every few weeks. We became such regulars, they stopped charging us for repairs. They seemed to grow quite attached to Joshua and chalked him up as an exception. Bending, breaking, or losing his glasses was just part of who he was. Joshua didn't know how to take care of things. He had cultivated no sense of pride about himself or his belongings. His "a little is good enough" attitude was apparent. There was no inner sense of striving to do his very best or complete anything. He was also developing an attitude of self-entitlement. He felt he was owed certain things. His belief seemed to be that everything could be replaced, so there was no need to take care of what belonged to him or anyone else. He was rough on himself, believing at the root that he was replaceable as well.

The triangulation between John, Joshua, and me continued to escalate. This child was so adept at manipulation that half the time we didn't know we'd been spun around and whipped to the ground until after it happened. That's when he proved just how intelligent he really was. Joshua was well versed in worldly survivor skills. In order to stay alive in his birth home, he had mastered lying, cheating, stealing, and doing whatever was necessary to keep things in constant consternation and under his control. And yet, Joshua could turn it around and show you his sweet self that so desperately reached out for love. As he continued to mistrust our love, we kept loving him. Our hope was that in time he would pick up on the rhythm and balance of accepting boundaries along with receiving our love. He could look at us and lie through those deep brown eyes like nobody's business. His refusal to recognize and respect boundaries, show fear, and manipulate less made parenting Joshua exhausting and depleting. We kept believing this would all pay off when Joshua learned to love himself. It would be worth all the effort if we could convince him how much he was worthy of love.

Jeffrey was most affected by the disturbance in our home. He had the black and white of right and wrong in him, and loved the structure of rules and the ordinary and predictable. It was very frustrating for him to watch the mom he loved being treated like this by another child in our family. He disliked the turmoil that existed between our walls now. I didn't dare lift my foot off the brakes or take my eyes off of Joshua for any length of time for fear that he would slide further backward. In doing so, my other three children were put on the back shelf many times. They certainly didn't deserve to become casualties.

Because Elizabeth and Ondrea were older, they could see that what I was doing was for the good of Joshua and our whole family, even though it looked like a battlefield much of the time. I couldn't give up the fight, or we would lose Joshua. We knew that Joshua still had a lot of issues to work through. Thankfully, he never fought us on therapy sessions, even as he grew into his middle school years. He continued to be cooperative and brave enough to look into the traumatic events of his past and face them head on. Never asking him what had been discussed, I was grateful he went for help.

Our boys had very different experiences academically. Joshua had an amazingly good year in his kindergarten year at Longfellow. This would continue throughout the next seven years, as Joshua had a curiosity and ability to learn quickly that helped him ride it through. He loved to learn and to read, and school was a good place in his mind.

First grade for Jeffrey had gone relatively well too, with a teacher who provided the structure and boundaries of a secure learning environment. Second grade was a good experience with a teacher who made kindness and learning look easy. Although she never had children of her own, she took each student under her wing to ensure success. Because we lived so close, in the spring I agreed to let him ride his bike to and from school. He had been riding bike since the age of four, and was very trustworthy. Joshua stayed with me in the classroom after school, and I was literally two to three minutes away. I felt Jeffrey would benefit from 20 minutes of quiet time to decompress. He handled this privilege responsibly....until one day.

Jeffrey had a thing about keeping his hair short, and remembering that school pictures were scheduled for the following day he decided to make his hair a little shorter. Using his dad's razor, he attempted to give himself a stylish "flat top". When I came home, I was greeted by small gobs of brown hair on the white tiled floor in the entryway and hallway. Jeffrey sheepishly showed me his new style, and we immediately left for the closest barbershop to rectify his new "flat top" before picture day. Everything could be fixed except for the bald skunk stripe down the center of his scalp. School photographers are amazing, and his school picture actually turned out quite cute. Only we knew the story behind it.

Another school year began, and Jeffrey ended up with a group of boys who together created a big challenge for their very seasoned third grade teacher. For years after she called this her "nightmare year" of five decades of teaching. She loved music, and to calm them down she would gather the students around her upright piano for singing sessions. Need I say more? Some of these rambunctious boys were slick and smooth and could hide their behavior behind others, but not my Jeffrey. He could not figure out how to pull himself in and out of the fray fast enough to avoid getting busted. Almost daily, she would send six or seven boys down to the office to see if the principal could turn them around and send them back for some quality learning. The cards were stacked against this marvelous teacher. Fourth, fifth, and sixth grades were acceptable years of learning for both of our boys, with some learning challenges for Jeffrey.

When Jeffrey entered junior high school, his frustration with lecture-style learning grew. He was officially diagnosed with an auditory processing deficit and auditory memory deficits by a skilled speech and language pathologist. He was highly visual and needed to learn that way to succeed in school. He needed to see the big picture first, then the details, which is totally the opposite of the widely used lecture method that feeds facts leading to the whole picture. Once he was given a 504 plan, he was able to get some modifications that better adapted to his learning style. After teaching children with learning differences all day, my evenings were a continuation of my school day. I taught Jeffrey lessons again in more visual ways. But I was his mom, not his teacher, and the struggle was real. With some improvement on classroom tests, his above-average intelligence finally was able to show through. Jeffrey's strong work ethic and determination became huge factors in his success later in life.

Solidifying my role, I continued as Jeffrey's number one interpreter and advocate. Due to my knowledge of student rights, and my work with children with learning differences, I made sure he continued to receive the accommodations for which he qualified. Sometimes it took my voice to make that happen. Even through his college years, I continued to translate his coursework into a visual format to ready him for exams. I was so proud when he received his degree in Computer Management from North Dakota State University. God had prepared me to help Jeffrey to succeed in learning.

Joshua was a very bright and capable student. Due to the addictions of his birth parents, Joshua had some of the characteristics of Fetal Alcohol Syndrome Effects. His very impulsive nature and inattentiveness made absorbing new information challenging. He liked being around other kids and was very smart, so learning was not particularly a challenge—but organizing himself and remembering to hand in his assignments was tough for him. With his impulsivity, letting him have the reins to make choices was seldom wise or in his best interest. I needed to help him stay in control and was terrified of the day when he would reclaim it. I knew the guidelines we insisted he follow were virtually saving his life, even though he fought them at every turn.

We had only a couple of photos to share with Joshua. One was a small five-inch photo of Joshua, his oldest brother, and his birth mother and father. The other appeared to be of infant Joshua at a baby shower. I had the strong feeling we were missing important pieces. Our social worker confided in me that the abuse that took place in the home of Joshua and his birth brothers was some of the worst ever seen in the county. It frightened me to think that even more horrific facts were yet to be discovered. When I asked, the adoption agency agreed to let me read through Joshua's complete file. Joshua was in therapy, and John and I felt we had made progress ourselves processing the abuse that we already knew about. Now, we were about to discover the true extent of abuse and neglect that Joshua had suffered while in his birth home. I wanted to put all the pieces of the puzzle together, but I was afraid that even after finding them, it might be impossible to put our own little Humpty-Dumpty back together again.

The social worker was correct. The abuse was hideous and heart-breaking. Part way through, I couldn't read one more horrible word. I shut the file, handed it to the receptionist, and walked out the door completely shocked. From that point on, we had to work with what we knew, and we were forced to broaden our understanding to include the unthinkable. Being told that the agency thought it best to split the boys up should have been a huge red flag. At various times, they had been placed into three separate adoptive homes in different parts of the state. Joshua's brown eyes had seen and experienced way too much during his earliest years, years that could have made all the difference to him. We had arrived too late. All we could do was to attempt to go back and build bridges and repair hurts. We could only hope that Joshua would reach out and take the rope we had thrown to bring him safely ashore.

Joshua had called us Mom and Dad since the first time we had pulled into our driveway. I was so encouraged by this. I thought this might be an indication of the possibility of a real bond between us. At first, our growing family did meld together, but our family life changed when Joshua joined us. This is hard for me to admit. Like a wool sweater that's been washed in hot water, our family life had lost its original shape. There was no stretching it back to the way it was. Our family would for-ever forward have a new and different shape, one not conducive to cre-ating the tight-knit family of four children we had hoped for. Not seeing your children bond was the most heartbreaking thing for me as a mother. I wanted so much to love them all into loving each other, and I fell short.

When the boys were six and seven, we acquired a family lake cab-in after the fatal accident that claimed John's mother and father. Every Friday night, we would pack up and head to the lake for the weekend. Many good memories were made in that humble, century-old place. Joshua was like a fish in water. He also loved sliding through puddles af-ter a hard rain and spending time adding on to his tree fort in the woods. He was a boy who explored nature with his curiosity and wondrous sense of imagination. He knew no boredom.

Eventually, Joshua's asthma and loose joint issues began to affect his ability to participate in contact sports. In high school he joined the swim team, where he lettered. At the same time, Jeffrey, who already played soccer, track, football, and hockey, started to excel in baseball as a left-handed pitcher. He played this sport from the age of nine through high school and American Legion. His baseball talents won him a look by professional scouts and college prospects, and he accepted a baseball scholarship to North Dakota State University. Unfortunately, unsuccessful recovery from surgery on a shoulder injury shut down his baseball career. This was a very difficult loss for Jeffrey to accept. From the time he was very young, he had envisioned himself playing baseball at the college level and beyond. As parents, it was so difficult to stand by helplessly as our child's hopes and dreams were shattered. His eventual acceptance and ability to shift his personal goals was remarkable to witness.

Meanwhile, Joshua began spreading his wings socially, spending most of his time with friends. His artistic skills had surfaced, and he became a talented clay sculptor and artist. He was amazing with his creative hands. In junior high and high school, his efforts won him ribbons in art shows. But it was clear to see that the personality differences between our boys were growing deeper as time went on. Sociability was not Jeffrey's strength, and his temporary friendships had a pattern of changing with whatever sport he currently participated in. His outside circle was small. Work, school, and home occupied most of his free time. Our family pets were always therapeutic for Jeffrey. He seemed to emulate much of their unconditional love and non- judgmental nature.

Once a year, we met up with Joshua's birth brothers. John even arranged a hunting trip near the Badlands with Joshua's older brother. They had a very close bond. Joshua's heart was devastated when his brother took his life at the young age of 19. Later, Joshua would have his brother's name tattooed across his chest near his heart. Looking back, it seems like the beginning of the end for Joshua.

When I wanted to get a true estimate of how Joshua was handling his world, I needed only to read his eyes. The big deep brown eyes I loved so much told such a story, and the more I gazed into them the deeper I seemed to get into his soul. They revealed his inner state of mind. Often what I saw was unsettling and sadly unfixable. After the death of his birth brother, his eyes began to lose their sparkle.

About the same time, Joshua's friend circle began to narrow some, and I began to see some subtle hesitancy and pulling away in him. When he entered high school, more blankness appeared in those brown eyes. Was it anger, confusion, or thoughts of hurt and past trauma? Outwardly, he kept trying his best to just be who he always was, but a flatness now dulled his once-bright eyes. It was as if a switch had been turned off. It was painful to see the light of hope leaving his eyes. Where was the resilience that he showed time after time? Where was that sense of eternal joy that had shined through?

In the middle of these changes came a rise in rebelliousness and projected anger. On good days, Joshua had brought so much love and joy to our family. But, now I was exhausted from my more difficult mission to guard him and to stay ahead of his quick thinking. My main charge throughout his childhood had been to keep him safe. He continued to be a risk taker, comfortable living on the edge and making impulsive decisions. Now that he was approaching 18, being his 24/7 protection service was harder. I worried incessantly about his safety, but I was no longer a voice Joshua listened to. The social worker had told us that Joshua would always have a four-year maturational delay from his chronological age. I dreaded him turning 18 with the maturity of a 14-year old.

After graduation, anxiety and alcohol seemed to consume Joshua. There were nights he didn't come home. When I did see his size 15 white sneakers by the back door, I was so relieved. His life seemed to be going off the rails. I was very afraid for his wellbeing and safety. He continued to work at a downtown family-owned pizza shop, and eventually rented an apartment upstairs. Meanwhile, we were encouraging him to consider furthering his education at one of the local universities. After a couple of expensive attempts, it was clear that his heart and mind were not engaged in college. We withdrew our offer to pay for further courses. Joshua meanwhile had taken a more lucrative job working nights as a warehouse manager, at a paper wholesale supplier. I was hopeful that this schedule might diminish his desire to spend free time with alcohol.

We saw less and less of him. He was roaming, vulnerably exposed to the world and every wild freedom in it. Many of the choices he made were less than desirable and sometimes risky. The next few years would include three DUIs, two within a month. He totaled our family car going 60 mph through a residential area with a lethal 0.30 alcohol level, rear-ending our neighborhood county sheriff. The next day, I found myself visiting a place that I had never been before...the local jail. I came to bail out my son, who was not remorseful, but angry and most likely still drunk. Fortunately, or maybe unfortunately, he got off easy, losing his driver's license for only three months. We were so grateful that everyone involved had escaped injury. In order for him to live with us, his only option was to enter an outpatient alcohol treatment program. He half-heartedly agreed.

Joshua and I were interviewed separately at the treatment center. I spoke to the male RN who had interviewed Joshua. This experienced RN was up front with me, saying that he could see right through Joshua and didn't believe for a minute he was being truthful. I took this as a bad omen, as it was a rare person who could see through my son's manipulation and charm. Joshua attended group meetings sporadically, while I dutifully showed up for my weekly parent meetings. John was out of town on Wednesday nights, so I usually attended solo. On one crucial meeting night, Joshua was supposed to join my parent group so that I could share my heartfelt letter explaining how his use of alcohol had impacted me and my life. I had called to remind him a few times, so he wouldn't forget. He failed to show. I was not surprised, but extremely hurt and disappointed. I felt this might be my last opportunity to air how I felt inside.

Joshua abruptly decided to discontinue his insincere commitment to get sober with the outpatient rehab program. The reins of control were once more in his own hands. Treatment was his ultimatum, and he blew off his family and his only chance.

Not long after, he disappeared from our home and from our lives, leaving behind strained relationships with our whole family. It was then that I clearly realized that our relationship had become quite symbiotic. Mothers want their children to be safe. I had tried so hard to defend and protect my vulnerable child from all the negative forces that lurked around every corner. Unconsciously, I attempted to bind my life to his in an effort to have better control over his risky and dangerous behaviors.

With every good intention in my heart, I had taken on an impossible task. I was very aware that I had to release him now both physically and emotionally, knowing that his choices were never mine to make. I felt defeated and that I had failed my son and myself. Tentatively, I moved forward from day to day, waiting for news I didn't want. It was a heart-wrenching time. The girls were on their own by then, and Jeffrey seemed relieved to have the chaos walk out the door with Joshua.

For two years, we had no idea of his whereabouts. We were aware that Joshua had lost his job at the warehouse and quite sure that he was spinning out of control wherever he had found shelter. Now of legal age, he had traded his family for a life with alcohol abuse that he had shown minimal ability to regulate. I felt betrayed and helpless with worry and cried myself to sleep countless nights wondering where he was and if he was even alive. My only solace was knowing Joshua had always been a survivor. When I couldn't take one more day of worry, I stepped up my search to find him.

Running into people who knew my son, I learned that he had been couch surfing in some sketchy places with even sketchier people. Finally I learned that he had moved in with a brother of a high school friend and had changed jobs. I parked myself by the stockroom doors at the rear of the outlet store where he worked. After a while, a warehouse employee walked out. I asked her to see if Joshua was working in the back room and if so to tell him someone was there to see him. My heart was in my throat as I waited. Suddenly Joshua was standing in front of me. My immediate reaction was a mixture of relief and gratefulness, and it was soon clear that Joshua was not overly pleased to see me. His words tumbled out quickly to make sure I knew how irritated and angry he was with me. Counseling had somewhat prepared me for the possibility of Joshua displacing his anger toward his birth mother on me. I also accepted that some of his anger was meant for me. I pleaded with him to meet me for lunch so we could talk things through. He agreed rather easily. I prepared myself for the possibility that he wouldn't show, but he did. As we started talking, his face softened, and I could tell that at some level, he was relieved to reconnect. When he hugged me before we parted, my relief soared.

Throughout our years with Joshua, John and I supported him to the ends of the earth. We were there for him in the good times and the bad. We loved the whole of our son. From around the age of 22, we remained in touch and Joshua saw us more frequently. Our relationship was mending, and my heart was also. A healthier closeness started to blossom between us, and my thoughts were in a much better place. Joshua was dating a co-worker, and they ended up moving to a small outlying town to live with her parents. He worked in their greenhouse on weekends in lieu of rent. When they moved into an apartment together it became apparent that their relationship was impaired by out-of-control drinking and marijuana use. After a blow-up, Joshua and his girlfriend ended their relationship, and he decided to move home temporarily as he was out of funds and had nowhere else to go.

It was about this time that he told me about another girl at work that he had wanted to ask out for a long time. He talked about Robin with such respect and high regard, and I urged him to reach out to her. She sounded like a beautiful girl inside and out. When Robin agreed to go out with him, he was thrilled. Could it be true, or was I imagining, that the light started to return to his beautiful brown eyes? Joshua was a different person when he was with Robin. They began a committed relationship that seemed lasting. His anxiety lessened some and eventually, because of Robin, he was able to let down the walls and feel the unconditional love that he had been seeking but feared all his life. She loved him for the wonderful man he had become, despite his human frailties. As Robin continued to give Joshua the gift of her encompassing love, he finally seemed to be open to trust. We can never repay her for that. His heart had been opened and the joy and hope he had lost over some difficult years had returned. He began showing up with Robin for more family occasions, and bridges were crossed to restore our family relationships. The closeness with him felt nothing short of a soothing balm on my hurting heart. I had my boy back.

But pain was an issue. Because of his abusive early childhood, his pain threshold was high. He could tolerate pain that he never fully shared with others. Joshua was tall, lanky, and had flat arches and joints that were more than flexible. On countless occasions, we saw Joshua pop his own shoulder and his knee joints back in place with no medical assistance. In high school, when doctors had checked his joint health, they ruled out a syndrome called Ehlers Danlos, which can affect the root of the aorta and often causes symptomless young athletes to die mid-game. Instead they determined that his weak immune system seemed to leave him vulnerable to joint pain and illness. The bottom line was that he had to quit contact sports. Now, in his twenties, his pain was becoming an even larger issue. He continued to hold a job, medicating his pain with prescription pills and alcohol.

Eventually, the pain in his ankles became unbearable, and affected his ability to walk. After a painful surgery to fuse his ankle and rebuild his arch, his walking improved but before long his entire body became affected by inflammation and pain. Joshua then suffered from a serious bout of psoriatic arthritis that created huge blistery sores all over his body. When he lost strength in his hands and began dealing with unremitting chronic pain, he was forced to seek full disability. He was always so good with his hands, and now he couldn't use them. Everything he loved to do was being taken away.

Joshua was immobile most of the time. Pain made sleep nearly impossible. He would go for days at a time with no sleep. He was on several pain medications, but his body was losing its strength and ability to cope. All the emotional pain he had endured in his early years now began to reopen and haunt him. His hope was fading. No type, combination, or amount of medication could relieve him from the horrendous stabbing pain that ravaged his body 24 hours a day. As a last-ditch effort, he was referred for evaluation to doctors at the Mayo Clinic in Rochester, Minnesota. We hoped beyond hope for a new suggestion or change in the treatment. When they had no new treatment suggestions for him, Joshua was devastated. It was later thought that Joshua may have been afflicted with Complex Regional Pain Syndrome, often set off after an orthopedic surgery.

His panic and desperation increased with every passing painful day and night. I could do nothing but watch him suffer. It was destroying me inside, as I had always been the one to guide him and encourage him not to quit. This time, my hands and words were useless. I could not help my son. Every door was slamming around him. I began to feel overwhelmed by my own helplessness, and worried about the emotional effects of all the pain and suffering on my son. Joshua didn't deserve more pain. He and Robin became engaged, and Joshua's spirits lifted some when they began to make plans for marriage and a possible family down the road. But the pain cast a shadow on that too.

He began calling me at odd hours, and we had some "pain pill" conversations that could be delusional. He was reaching out to me for answers, but my inability to distract and encourage him was wearing me down. No longer could I play the role of cheerleader. What had pain's affliction done to Joshua's curiosity in life, quickness of wit, contagious sense of humor, bright intelligence, artistic hands, gentleness, and most of all his resilience? His resilience had always shone like a shining light before him. It led him through the darkest of times, helping him forgive the wrongs of his broken past and to see beyond the now.

Friday, March 27, 2015, was the last time I spoke with Joshua. I knew he was seeking some version of encouragement, but there were none to be retrieved from the bone dry well inside me. I had no magical answers. Only hopelessness and worry swirled around inside me. I cut our conversation short by telling Joshua that I wasn't feeling the best and would call him on Monday. Early on Monday, March 30, my cell phone rang while I was having my morning coffee. It was Robin. She was crying so hard, I could barely understand her. But the words "Joshua shot himself!" were immediately seared forever into my brain. Time stood still as I tried to process what she had told me. She asked us to meet her at the hospital emergency room in Fargo. John had no words either, only tears. We contacted our other three children. It felt like we were both moving in slow motion, trying to prepare our minds for what would soon become our worst nightmare. The hospital was a little over an hour from our lake home. We were silent in the car. Clutching my cell phone in my lap, I prayed harder than I had ever prayed before. Enroute to Fargo, my phone rang again. Robin informed us that although our beautiful Joshua's pulse had returned for a very brief time, the ER staff was unable to save him. I turned off my phone without saying goodbye and stared straight ahead in shock. How could I ever survive the loss of another child?

When I made my wild-eyed entrance into the ER, our daughter Elizabeth was already there with Robin. The sheriff filled us in on the circumstances. Joshua had shot himself in the side of his temple. I could barely breathe, but I had to deal with my swirling emotions in full view of everyone in the waiting room. Inconsolable, I wanted to crawl into a dark cave and never come out. Robin was giving a detective information concerning the events that led up to the shooting. When Joshua was prepared to be viewed, the nurse led John and me through a set of closed doors.

I was sure I had been directed into the wrong room. But as I stared more intently at the face and the body that lay draped in white sheets, I knew I had found my boy. The beautiful eyes that had always been a window for me were no longer recognizable, as they were bulged out from the pressure of the gun shot to his head. I hugged him and sobbed violently, unable to grasp this reality. I did not want to believe that my boy would make the decision to leave this world on his own. I told him over and over that I forgave him, and that I understood that he couldn't stay on this earth where there were no answers to end his pain. In the end, only God could save him. I wanted to stay with him forever, if possible. But my husband finally convinced me it was time to leave. I patted the bony knees that were the reason he never wanted to wear shorts, and John held and patted his precious flat feet as we said our last goodbyes. I tried to drink in this last image of my son. Ironically, Joshua had signed up some years earlier to become a donor. But the only part of Joshua that could be donated were the corneas from those beautiful brown eyes. Now they could become a window for somebody else.

The complicated emotions of my son's death by suicide decimated my spirit. Once again, I was forced to face the death of parental dreams. I wanted to give the world to my son. Knowing that Joshua was not in pain and wasn't suffering anymore gave me some solace. I recalled his adoption social worker sharing once that even at the age of five, Joshua was on a fast path toward self-destruction and his life expectancy may have been as brief as ten years had he not found a family to love him. The fact that love and luck kept him with us until the age of 33 was probably the biggest miracle we could have hoped for.

We held a loving goodbye for him at a well-attended memorial service. We wanted people to know that our family held no shame around suicide. Joshua didn't want to die. He only wanted his pain to end. It was his solution in a really dark time and was the one act that Joshua knew for sure would stop his unbearable pain. Writing my own son's obituary, I opened wide my soul's gates, and the words flowed through my tears onto paper. I felt no one knew the whole of him like I did. Although it was very difficult to do this as his mother, I viewed authoring it as an honor.

Some weeks later, we finally received his autopsy report. I was shocked to read that there were no pain medications, no drugs, and no alcohol in his system at the time of his death. Nothing! It was one more painful proof of his attempt to use his own efforts and resiliency one last time to pull himself out of his pain. I wondered if his body being totally clean of substances might have been his final gift of respect to us. Still, the autopsy information sent me to a deeper level of sadness, realizing he left this world having made every possible attempt to change his circumstances. Defeat and total loss of hope finally beat him down. He was desperate. Thank you, Joshua, for teaching me through it all more about resiliency than anyone else could. You were valiant in your renewed efforts and tried everything humanly possible to change the unchangeable.

The next few months left me with many unanswered and haunting questions. I visited the Moorhead Police Department to try to speak to an officer who had been in attendance at the scene of Joshua's suicide. I was a mother on a mission and nothing could stop me. Unfortunately, none of those involved were in the office or on duty, so I sat down with another officer who gave me a copy of the police report. Reviewing the lead officer's documentation of events that culminated in Joshua taking his life was brutal. A copy remains in our safety deposit box, although I have never had the courage or the desire to reread it. It is truth in safe-keeping.

I learned that as the SWAT team tried to talk him down, Joshua told them that this moment had been coming for a long time. I will always wonder whether there was any chance that I could have persuaded him to stay. But in my heart, I knew that wasn't possible. I could not have tried harder or poured more love into Joshua. I never gave up on him, and he knew he was loved. I drank in the words he wrote on a Mother's Day card given to me the year before his death: *"You are the best mom ever, and I love you. I could never have had a better mother than you, Mom."* I live on, remembering those words.

Knowing for certain that there wasn't one more thing I could have said or done to save him, is the only thing that allows me to feel no guilt, only deep sadness. Our challenging attempts to help him had not been in vain and remained a comfort to me. Flooded with sorrow and deeply in grief, I also worried about his beautiful fiancée Robin and tried to support her as much as I was able. It was a very low and confusing valley in my life. And once again I was handling my grief very differently than John. While I was reaching out for help and understanding, he was pulling in his sorrow to lock the love and memories of his son deep within. They were safe there. I sought more knowledge about death by suicide through reading every book I could about being a survivor of suicide. I attended weekly meetings of a local suicide grief support group. There was power in telling my story there once again, but my spirit was restless and pushed me to move on in my grief search. I have a special kinship with those who have lost a loved one to suicide. It is an extremely complicated death to process and accept that is not easily explained.

A few weeks later, as John and I were walking our Labrador puppy Bleu on the bike trail, we came upon a friendly couple. Our husbands broke off into their own conversation, while Mary and I moved on to topics of our own. Somehow I circled around to the recent death of our son by suicide. Mary compassionately understood my grief, as she had lost her brother by suicide several years earlier. We talked for over an hour on the bike path, and it was so comforting to be fully understood. Mary and I decided we absolutely needed to take this conversation to the next level over a cup of coffee. A couple of difficult weeks later, I worked up the courage to call Mary and set up our coffee date. I am so grateful I followed through, as today I continue to be blessed with her beautiful friendship. We have each crossed some rough waters, and Mary has been my savior when I didn't know whether I could survive. God can literally place people on your path when you need them. This was no coincidence. Together we have each learned to walk around and through some significant life losses, knowing we have each other's support.

Another caring friend, Jill, sent me a gift certificate to see Mariah, a well-known local holistic teacher of yoga, an energy healer, and a shamanic practitioner who claimed success in guiding individuals through personal transformation. I was open to anything and everything that would help me move out of my inner pain.

On May 8, 2015, just five weeks, three days, seven hours, and 30 minutes after Joshua's self-inflicted gunshot wound, I arrived for a healing session with Mariah. I was struggling to make sense of my detonated world and desperate for something to provide an anchor for my untethered mind. Pulling up to a brown bi-level house overlooking a huge lake, I felt curious and apprehensive. I was greeted by a youngish, slender-built yogi with curly auburn hair and kind eyes. I was open and optimistic to the idea of receiving some sort of healing of mind, body, or spirit. Never did I imagine I would be gifted with all three.

Mariah gave me a brief rundown of what I could expect. There would be no physical contact with my body once the session began. Mariah busied herself about the room and around me on the table in preparation for the arrival of my spiritual guides who were being called. I was encouraged not to prejudge or analyze what was happening and to keep an open and accepting mind. Inhaling the bitter and lingering sage that Mariah swirled around me, I closed my eyes, and began to relax. I sank deep into the comfort of the table. Almost instantly I felt tears trickling from the outside corners of my eyes, and I was overwhelmed with the desire to see my mother. This feeling was soon followed by a magnificent intense violet light. It began to emit quick pulses of black. I recognized this nondescript violet as my mother's spirit, and I called to her wildly from within. I conveyed to her how much I needed her now in my sadness and how much I missed her presence on earth. Her energy light stayed close and was steadily intense and unwavering, as if to hold my spirit and prepare me for what was to follow.

I remember feeling a little surprised and disappointed that I had not immediately experienced the spiritual presence of my son Joshua. Then in the snap of a finger, there he was, seated on a large brown boulder. "Hi, Mom," he said, in an unassuming voice that was unquestionably his, the one he had greeted me with so often through the years. In a state of unbelievable joy, I drank in his image with my eyes. Joshua was dressed in an ultra-vibrant blue tee shirt with short sleeves and a blurred tan garment covering his legs. His size 15 bare feet poked out below him, dangling over the front of the boulder. I inhaled the beauty of the handsome chiseled face that I loved so much. His eyes held the look of remorse, the same expression he used right before he had been caught red-handed in one of his mischievous capers. His brown eyes avoided mine until he looked straight into my eyes and said, "I'm sorry".

I wailed and screamed with internal emotion, "Oh Josh, why did you do it?"

Staring straight at me, he replied softly, "I don't know." His words were framed with a sense of honest regret, and his body language and demeanor reaffirmed that his impulsivity had indeed played a detrimental part in his decision to pull the trigger. Next, with deep sincerity, he said "Thank you".

"Are you out of your pain?" I asked, hopefully.

"Yes, look!" Joshua said, as he stood up to do an impromptu jig-like dance. Goofy things he did like that had always made me laugh.

"Are you happy now?" I continued.

"Yes!" he responded, the broadest and most genuine smile possible upon his beautiful face.

Then I noticed a white bundle of playful energy in the lower left corner of my vision. Right away I recognized it as the spirit of our infant son John Ryan, the baby brother that Joshua never had the chance to meet. John Ryan was just a presence, never speaking and yet transmitting limitless joy in a freely moving and nonstop way. His worldly body would never have been capable of this energetic movement and pure happiness shot throughout my body.

Next, three siblings who had passed over the years appeared one by one to thank me for very particular reasons. My dad appeared toward the end of this vision to apologize for hurtful things he had said. Then my husband's deceased parents appeared with silent, smiling faces, like rolling credits at the end of a movie. As they leaned into one another, the message of their smiles was one of wise reassurance. My mother-in-law Helen was a great support for me as a young wife and mother. Next my maternal and soft-spoken grandmother Melissa floated into my sight. "Gran" flashed her ever-hesitant half smile, which washed over me with endearment. As she smiled at me, her cute dimples broke through as if they were unable to be contained.

The last to appear was my dear friend Joan, who I lost to cancer. She and I had taught in the same school at different grade levels but in adjacent classrooms. We were there for each other every morning as we greeted our students, offering an empathetic ear as we recounted dilemmas and worries regarding our sons. We freely shared raw thoughts and events that we didn't share with our spouses. We formed a common bond of trust and understanding and were shoulders of support for each other when one of us had seemingly lost hope. Most important, we made each other laugh. When Joan's cancer came back, I had the honor of being a part of her journey as she readied herself to die. I felt her loss in a powerful way, and I continue to miss her in my life. That she would appear to me now made sense. Her smile was bright and happy, and it conveyed a silent message of eternal peaceful comfort that she so well deserved.

Toward the end of my session, my mother's incredible spirit returned. She had gifted me by gathering all those I needed now in order to receive healing. As she faded from my sight, the tops of my feet began itching intensely. It felt like they were covered by a dense blanket of viciously biting mosquitoes in the thick of summer. This uncomfortable sensation brought me back to reality quickly, and all that had appeared spiritually faded from my sight. I knew that I had just experienced life-changing moments, ethereal and earthly at the same time. Mariah softly touched my shoulder to indicate our healing session had come to an end and I should gather myself and my things and meet her upstairs, when I was ready, to debrief my healing session. Wordless for a few minutes as I sipped a glass of cold water, I took a seat beside her and began to unravel what I had just experienced. I don't usually cry, and the tears that rolled out of my eyes surprised me. I tried to recall each moment in a clear and authentic way. I didn't want to forget a single detail.

Scribbling down my words on a tablet, Mariah interjected that during my healing session, there was quite a gathering of people from my spirit family. Mariah shared that my spirit guides left a message for me. They wanted me to know that I must keep my feet on this earth for now, and that I had important things to accomplish here. They wanted me to dance by the water and once again feel joy in my life here on earth. This reference toward dancing by the water struck me as very uncanny. I have always been strongly drawn toward water to receive its peace and healing when my mind is at unrest.

My guides identified my spirit animal as the starfish. I found this choice to be a comfortable and curious one. In addition to love, the starfish also holds the characteristics of guidance, vigilance, inspiration, brilliance and intuition. The starfish spirit animal is said to teach a person to cure themselves over time, fill up the void, and replace it with something better. It symbolizes regeneration, renewal, and self-sustainability.

Coincidentally, a few weeks after my session with Mariah, the water began to call to me. Before Joshua's death, I had purchased a plane ticket to visit my sister Nancy, who was living and working in Naples, Florida. However, given our recent tragedy I didn't feel I could go. With the encouragement of both my husband and my sister, I decided to follow through with my travel plans. I would use my time by the water to rest and try to process some of the grief that was devouring me. Each day after my sister left for work, I loaded up my beach bag and hat and drove my rental car to Lowdermilk Beach with no agenda but to let the sea's waves lull me into some sort of hypnotizing peace. Each new morning brought me closer to my last goodbye to the ocean. I strolled barefoot, my feet absorbing the heated softness of the sand.

As I was contemplating the starfish as my spirit animal, my mind leaped to the well-known story of the starfish. It tells about a young man seen on the shore carefully picking up and gently tossing every starfish back into the waiting arms of the sea.

Noticing the young boy's actions from a distance, an elderly gentleman closed in on the young boy and asked, "What are you doing? You will never be able to save every single starfish washed ashore! There are too many."

To that, the young boy replied, "If I can save but one starfish, then it will all be worth my while."

Reflecting on this beautiful story, I realized that Joshua was that one precious starfish we were called to save, and every bit of effort had been worthwhile. Each day at the beach, I looked for starfish washed ashore, and each day I came up empty handed. After I left the beach, I looked for starfish jewelry and the perfect starfish urn for my son's ashes. . The starfish was a direct messenger of connection with my son, and finding and buying a silver urn calmed the angst that lived in my bones.

The day before I was to leave my healing haven by the water, I went to the sea one last time to say goodbye. As I crossed over the bridge leading to the beach, I stopped to breathe and take in the all of it: the blue-green water, the white shelled sand, and the welcoming warm breeze that embraced me once more. The water seemed to tug insistently at me, ushering me to a seat near the water's edge. After sinking into the warm and inviting sand, I grabbed my pen and journal, deeply inhaled the salty air, and began to spill my thoughts out on paper.

Taking breaks to walk along the seashore, I began to focus in on the beauty of the people that I passed, the sound of laughter, and the curiosity in the faces of wobbly toddlers playing at the water's edge and tipping over into the shifting white sand. All the while, the softly moving waves played their background music. My thoughts rolled in and out to the tempo of their movement. As I waded into the blue-green water, I felt perfectly synchronized with the rhythm of the waves. I let the ocean caress and hold me as I sat in the water. Could this be heaven? My eyes were still constantly searching for starfish. Soon it would be time to leave, but the ocean invited me to stay just a little longer.

Then a beautiful young boy with large brown eyes came out of nowhere and entered the water near me. He appeared to be about eight or nine and his lips formed a wide smile. Riding my direction on his boogey board, he looked directly at me and said, "Hi. I hope you're enjoying your day at the ocean." I thanked him as he paddled around me. He kept humming an unfamiliar tune as he circled me, and my eyes followed him as he headed deeper into the water. He seemed so comfortable with the sea as he continued to navigate his board in larger circular movements. Even after he passed, his eyes never broke their gaze on me, and the smile on his face never changed. That this young brown-eyed boy had singled me out in the water seemed unusual. Was it just my imagination that he seemed so fixated on me? I looked away for brief moments, but each time I turned around I was met again by his eyes. Then, an older man with gray hair and a kindly lined face walked toward the boy, opened his hand and said excitedly, "Look what I found! A starfish!" I was drawn to my feet and walked toward the man.

"You found a starfish?" I asked.

"Yes," he announced as he opened his hand. I could see this was a unique starfish with six or seven arms instead of the usual five. I was mesmerized by this beautiful creature.

"You're going to put it back, aren't you?" I asked.

"Yes, but first I'm going to show the children. There are all kinds of starfish out here. You should go out a little further and see them all," the man said, with wonder in his eyes. With that, he called the children on shore to wade toward him and look at his find.

I contemplated, just for a moment, going further out to see this magical spot. But I had never wandered quite that far from shore before. I remained absolutely gob smacked by the timing of this starfish event and felt so eerily connected with Joshua. As I sat back down, I let the waves wash me back to shore one last time. I had finally seen a starfish, and this one was alive. I slowly gathered my belongings and began walking toward the parking lot, never glancing back at this mystical body of water. The sea had given me a sense of knowing in all that had just taken place and had put a smile on my face. It had taken a young brown-eyed boy with a beautiful smile to draw me out to see the man's starfish. This could not have been a coincidence. As I got in the car and turned on the air conditioning, I thanked God for this amazing day by the water and for the gift of the boy, the man, and the starfish. My guides had indeed given me the perfect spirit animal, and this poem about the sea rolled out of me.

Until Next Time

Oh sea, you have a hold on me

Giving and taking energy in a never-ending circle,

Calming, strong, but never predictable.

Such it is with life outside the sea

With all its metamorphic changes

My grief struggle continued. After years of stress and worry about Joshua and Jeffrey, I had become a vulnerable target. Four months after Joshua's death, I was told I had breast cancer. During treatment, I had to turn my focus from Joshua's death onto myself. Fortunately, the cancer was caught in the early stages, and after a lumpectomy, 33 rounds of radiation, and a chemo pill for five years, I have remained seven years cancer free. Though my cancer diagnosis wasn't a blessing, it had the power to make self-care my first priority.

Grief had not left me, but I was successful in keeping it at bay some of the time. I also continued to express my feelings in writing. Joshua's amazing resilience and spirit stayed with me to guide me through the challenging moments of recovery. Who better to show me how resilience could be my best friend in difficult times? No matter how I tried, one haunting question remained to shadow over me....WHY was all this struggle and pain cast upon my son?

My Boy

My boy, my child, a light's gone out.

God, please take away my self-doubt.

Stay by my side son and be with me

And I promise to let your soul fly free!

Fly fast and high in the wind like a kite

And fan hope's flicker to make it shine bright.

Leave just a whisper of your essence behind

And know that forever you'll be in my mind.

You are my hope of life's light anew.

Your spirit revealing colors in every hue

Embed in my soul and send away sorrow,

To replace it with joy for a new tomorrow.

Words of love, Mom

From the Wild Water's Edge

How many times I stood watching you from the wild water's edge, with you just out of reach and me praying you to a safe place. Like a lifeguard, I stood ready to anticipate that action, those words, or that promise that would alert me to swim far out into the deep waters to safely bring you back to shore yet one more time.

Sadly, I must see the reality now, that these were but temporary saves. My heart was entwined with yours and you had become like an appendage that shared an unbreakable symbiotic bond with my soul. I pushed my way in through the smallest cracks of your vulnerability in order to give you boundaries, keep you safe, and give you love. You had learned to be a survivor at a most vulnerable young age and you knew how to change the truth to save your very life.

Mastering the ability to turn your emotions off with a switch, you became a chameleon, who could quickly assess the people around you and your surroundings, and change your color as needed. You knew every safety exit for a quick escape. I loved you to the depths of your soul and was determined to keep you in a place of acceptance that was tempered by expectation. I have cried thousands of every kind of tear for you, and dedicated myself to helping you believe in yourself, other people, and your own worthiness of love and hope. I gave you everything I had, and toward the end of your life, I came to the brutal realization that no matter the number of tears or the amount of trying, I was losing you. Too painful to carry in my heart or mind, I turned this thinking into the anxious refusal to predict a sad outcome. Nothing earthly had ever had the ability to convince you that your beautiful soul was worthy of unconditional love and acceptance and that your authentic self was perfect just as it was. But you were worth every attempt. In the end, you found your way to all of the things we so wanted for you. And we go on, loving and missing you now, filled with peace that you have found rest in the arms of God, who has held you through it all. Love you, Joshua...Mom

I remained trapped in the wreckage of loss and trying to find a way to piece together the remnants of my shattered soul. Suicide is a complicated type of death. With the loss of my son, I also experienced my own loss of personal competence. Self-doubt kept rearing its ugly head, feeding my hopelessness. After a lot of work with a therapist from the cancer center, I thankfully restored belief in myself again. Eventually I was plagued less by traumatic intrusive images from the last time I viewed my son. My ability to concentrate started to grow, opening the gate to many former activities and passions. Routine became my friend. Looking back, I can see all the push and pull and how far I have come in learning to appreciate that I did all a mother could do. I am so grateful I can see this now.

Joshua's death by suicide was complicated by the many different ways suicide is perceived. Now I understand how courage and risk are required to approach and show compassion to a parent of a son who took his life. People in our society appear to avoid the subject of suicide. I feel it should be talked about and recognized as an illness-related death. For survivors, the hurt and pain of tragic loss are real. Suicide is a horrible loss and brings with it confusion and complicated feelings. People need education on the topic of suicide to expand understanding. It starts with me and my lack of shame and guilt over this difficult death of a loved one.

I approached the fact that my son took his life with no shame. Over time, I looked for new ways of appreciating and feeling more comfortable with others. I have grown far more aware of the beauty of honest relationships and of the people who will add quality to my friendship circle. Fewer and truer can be better.

Life's inertia pushed me forward. My marriage and our remaining children were left to walk a rocky road at times. It was as if a bomb had blown apart our family. The absence of Joshua's magnetic energy in our lives remains difficult for all of us to this day. Our scars are far from healed and we still process his loss in different ways, all too hurtful to talk about together even eight years later. An invisible shield of privacy has always protected our individual losses, and none of us has the heart to remove our own shield or disrespect anyone else's. Like a sacred story, each of us was touched in our own personal way that needs to be honored.

Today, some of Joshua's ashes remain in the starfish urn. Given his boundless life energy, we felt that burying his remains underground would not be appropriate. For now, I still have part of him with me to protect and keep safe, though my intention is to spread some of him among the starfish on my next trip to the ocean. Some of his ashes have been returned to the lake and to the woods by his tree fort. Robin has had some of his ashes embedded in a beautiful tattoo on her forearm that says, "Never Give Up". My daughters and granddaughter Olivia also have meaningful tattoos as reminders that Joshua's spirit lives on. I am comforted knowing he has now become a part of people and places that he held dear.

Part Four

JEFFREY THOMAS MADDOCK:
The Model of Grace and Acceptance

People will forget what you said, people will forget what you did, but people will NEVER forget how you made them feel.

Maya Angelou

When Jeffrey joined us as an infant, he innately had a strong preference for quiet and calm. What he got instead were two sisters and two parents who seldom celebrated these qualities. As extroverts, we are all very outgoing people who love being in a crowd, and better yet being the center of attention and entertainment. When our clan is together, our collective energy and laughter is easily over the top. It is hard to sustain this kind of energy, but somehow, we manage to succeed. Actually, Jeffrey was somehow oddly entertained by our activity and openness. He took his place as one of us in his own quiet way. He was loved for who he needed to be and could not have been more wanted.

Jeffrey was competitive. He wanted to win. At six, playing soccer, he would often take over by playing all positions, and winning the game himself. But he also had difficulty in reading signals and body language of others, which limited his social activities and friendships. Because he was so loyal to each sport and naturally athletic, he became the best at each sport he played. He cared about pleasing himself and grew less interested in pleasing others. His focused desire allowed his sense of confidence to flourish.

Friendships were harder. Jeffrey chose to minimize the need for making himself vulnerable to the unreliable moving targets of peers and friendships. By removing this stressor from his life, his general acceptance of people could become uncomplicated and without the cloudiness of judgement. His great sense of pragmatism allowed him to accept his weaknesses in this area and move on. This trait of acceptance was evident when unsuccessful surgery for a shoulder injury ended his hopes and dreams of a future in baseball. Being a talented pitcher had become a core part of his identity. Watching him work through this loss was painful as a parent, and his impressive shift of focus to school and his future was a credit to his ability to accept what was and move forward.

When Jeffrey bravely reached out to the world of social dating in college, I was both encouraged and elated. Eventually, he met the woman he would become engaged to and marry. His heart took the chance, and it filled him with a new happiness and trust that I thought I'd never see. The future was his now. His ultimate accomplishment and win came with the birth of his beautiful son four years later. In his son lives that same amazing innocence and vulnerability that made Jeffrey so treasured.

As I write, it has only been a little over three years since Jeffrey's illness and death. My pain and memories are buried in a shallow layer within myself. They are in a state of partial peace. My grief this third time around has required me to dig deeper than I could ever have imagined possible. I felt the need to turn myself inside out to search for lasting hope and a livable state of peace. I have begged the universe openly for the grace and ability to find them. On my own, this would never have been possible. My mother heart was ripped open raw once again, and I knew I had to fight harder than ever to make the bleeding stop...if only a spurt at a time.

Yet I felt myself propelled by the desire to share my experience and what I learned from losing multiple children. Although the loss of Jeffrey is still painfully fresh, my wish to honor my son pushes me forward in this writing endeavor. Throughout this journey I have felt all three boys nudging me from another realm to summon the necessary emotional strength. My undying love and remarkable pride for these beautiful souls now lives within me, ever safe in my heart. With his love and guidance, I will tread lightly and lovingly around and through the memories of my gentle, truthful, and big-hearted Jeffrey who showed such courageous vulnerability and acceptance in what life had planned for him.

From the time he was very young, Jeffrey was always the picture of health, strength, and athleticism. That's why we were so shocked when, in March 2019, Jeffrey went to the Emergency Room with chest pain. At first, the doctors diagnosed pericarditis and possibly Epstein-Barr Syndrome. When they noticed some irregularities in his bloodwork, they became suspicious that there might be more factors at work. After he completed additional scans and tests at the hospital, he was released. No news was good news for three days, but on day four, he went to the clinic to discuss his test findings. We were in the middle of a Tuesday Bridge game at a nearby Holiday Inn when John received a phone call from Jeffrey. Returning with his phone in hand, he had me join him in a small lobby and turned on the speaker. I braced myself by leaning against a glass window, as Jeffrey asked us if we were sitting down. My insides vibrated with a sense of alarm, as in a teary voice Jeffrey shared that he had just been diagnosed with chronic myelogenous leukemia (CML) an uncommon cancer of the bone marrow.

I searched for words of motherly assurance and comfort and some-how found what my son needed to hear. John and I pledged to be there for him every step of the way. We were sure that with his young age and perfect record of health, helping to cheer Jeffrey along toward victory would be enough. Surely, he could take this beastly opponent down with relative ease. We believed that our hardworking, persevering, and logical son would face this physical challenge with characteristic determination and effort, as he had every other difficult thing in his life. Jeffrey refused to lose, and he was determined to call on every bit of strength he could muster to in order to kick this disease. And so, his soldiers were called in, and the battle began.

I remembered back to a promise Jeffrey made five years earlier that was now hanging precariously in the air. Leaving Joshua's funeral service on Jeffrey's arm, I told him how desperately I needed him. I begged him to promise that he would never leave me, because I could never survive the loss of any more of my children. He stared straight into my eyes and answered, "Mom, I am right here, and I'm not going to go anywhere."

After Joshua's death, I was again keenly aware of the fragility of life and what can happen in the blink of an eye. Jeffrey was now my only remaining son. This gentle soul had the steadiness of a rock in stormy waters, and I would need every bit of that steadiness to hold onto in the days and years ahead. It was inconceivable to me that this heartfelt promise coming from my always honest son might not be able to be kept. Our son, a grounding force in our family and the picture of strength and excellent health, had suddenly become a possible statistic to an aggressive leukemia in the prime of his life. There was no time to prepare for the battle we faced. Our boots hit the ground, fighting a battle that occupied the next year of our lives.

Looking back, I see visions of blurred chaos, heart-pounding fear, and what seemed like eternities of waiting. After a few weeks in Fargo, Jeffrey was accepted for treatment at the Mayo Clinic in Rochester, Minnesota, some 500 miles away. The plan was for Jeffrey to receive very powerful chemo treatments in hopes that the cancer would go into remission long enough for a bone marrow transplant. John, Jeffrey and I felt hopeful when we visited the Mayo campus to meet with doctors, and tour one of the two on-campus Gift of Life Transplant Houses. These huge historical homes offered a cost effective home-style environment for caregivers and their loved one who awaited a transplant. Each patient and their caregiver shared one private room equipped with two queen-sized beds, a closet, and a bathroom. We were given a cupboard for personal food items as well as the use of two commercial kitchens for meal preparation. Adjoining the kitchen was a large communal dining room, laundry facilities, a library, and a few family rooms with televisions spread about the three floors.

Going to Mayo meant Jeffrey would leave his family behind. This was extremely difficult for him. Because Jeffrey's son and wife had school and work obligations, we were honored to be able to help out as Jeffrey's primary caregivers. Spending this time with our son was a gift we will treasure forever. His amazing physicians were dedicated to bringing our son into the place of remission, making a bone marrow transplant possible. It was this transplant that would eventually offer him a new life, free of leukemia. Leaving his family behind was so difficult for Jeffrey. Their little boy was only five, and even with daily FaceTime sessions, it wasn't the same for his family. But, like the talented relief pitcher that Jeffrey had been, he now refocused his vision and targeted his energy on striking out and eradicating the disease that sought to steal home base and his life.

We settled into the Gift of Life House (GOL) and acclimated ourselves with what would become Jeffrey's new home for an extended period of time. His days were busy with multiple doctor appointments, chemo sessions, bloodwork, platelet infusions, blood transfusions, scans and frequent bone marrow biopsies. Days were grueling and fatiguing, but minutes passed quickly, so our minds couldn't get too far ahead of the present. Exhaustion caused both of us to collapse into our beds at night. My mothering skills were called upon to the fullest capacity as I shadowed him day and night. Still, there was nowhere else I could bear to be other than beside my son. Many nights I would be awakened as Jeffrey whimpered in his dreams. It was torture to hear him, because I couldn't run to him and hold him as I had when he was young. I would lie in the other bed imagining the havoc that all those chemo combinations were creating in his body in order to poison the illness out of him. Then, I would talk myself down by remembering that these toxins were his only hope.

But perhaps nothing brought the reality of his cancer home to me like the daily visits to the hospital pharmacy, where we waited with other pale and bald cancer patients and their loved ones for their cancer drugs. I said a prayer of thanks every day for Jeffrey's excellent health coverage, and I wondered how those not as fortunate managed the exorbitant costs of the medications they required. For Jeffrey, who could never easily swallow a pill of any size and fortunately rarely needed to do so, this was a new and foreign world. At night, I would stare from my bed at the dimly illuminated double shelves where 20-plus cancer drugs were neatly and ominously organized, all of them now part of his daily routine.

Soon after arriving at Mayo, he had his first chemo treatment. Jeffrey experienced a life-threatening reaction which caused his kidneys to shut down. Dialysis quickly joined his treatment regimen. It was an extremely scary time for all of us, as we hoped and prayed his kidney function would return before dialysis zapped all his strength. Our prayers were answered when, a few weeks later, his blood counts showed enough improvement that he could get rid of the three dialysis tubes implanted in his neck. My beautiful bald-headed Jeffrey referred to these multi-colored tubes as his "dreads". After this critical event, we never took a day of Jeffrey's treatment for granted. We had to live with erratic spontaneity, never knowing how his body would react, but thankfully from then on he was able to receive chemo with only occasional setbacks and infections.

While living in this world of medicine and illness, my compassion was profoundly impacted and changed forever. Healthy people go through life completely unaware and on a whole different plane than those who are chronically and critically affected by illness. Not by choice, we were surrounded by this new dimension, which I began to call the "World of the Sick". Everyone understands that people can get gravely ill. But I learned that unless forced to live in this world daily and breathe its air, this World of the Sick remains invisible, and not part of day-to-day reality for the masses. In this hidden world, I found a place where empathy abounds. Kindness and compassion flow so much more freely, enfolding those in the World of the Sick in a protective cocoon. People here live for the moment in a state of raw authenticity. They smile more frequently, and because they share similar emotions of the heart, they are more vulnerable and open to others. Their degree of approachability seems directly related to a desperate craving for human connection and places them into an accepting environment where skin color and cultural differences don't create barriers. In the World of the Sick, people become unified into one kind of humanity, a nurturing oneness that helps people survive together.

Such was the case with many of the special people that I had the blessing of meeting in that world. We found each other in the hallways, cafeterias, and family rooms of hospitals at all hours of the day and night. Our common connection penetrated like a laser through the membrane of another's soul. Many times, without even knowing it, these individuals became a temporary pillar of respite to lean upon. Names didn't matter in this world. It was only the essence of a person that spoke to our need. There was a good chance that I might never see these significant people again. Still, a single gesture or words shared often became an integral part of my grief and healing. In the transformational journey toward acceptance, these incidental exchanges profoundly influenced the "who" I am becoming.

I got to know Cindy, another GOL House resident. Her daughter Allie had recently received a heart transplant and they were from our hometown. Frequently we shared an early morning cup of coffee in the white rockers overlooking the flowers and implanted inspirational messages in the back yard of the GOL House. Cindy and I centered ourselves for busy days of back-to-back medical appointments, and we aired our frustrations and worries. Downtime is vital to those taking care of medically challenged loved ones. I cherished my mornings. I became friends with Cindy, and my downtrodden soul was thirsty for the positive energy she radiated. Several other amazing women were residing in the GOL house while their husbands, mothers, daughters, or sons were in various stages of receiving treatment and transplants. Together we rode the rollercoaster of fear and hope day after day. Some days, all we had to give each other was a smile as we made our way to our rooms after a long day and night at the hospital. Yet the smiles we received in return gave us so much encouragement and understanding.

Occasionally, when all was calm on the home front, a group of us would walk to the restaurant down the street for a quick evening glass of wine, a much-needed reprieve from the heaviness we constantly carried. Even though brief, escaping allowed us a chance to laugh and feel a sense of normalcy and also renewed us with group hope and connection. I remain in contact with most of these women today, and I continue to think of them and their admirable courage and devotion.

In the fall of 2019, Jeffrey underwent genetic testing. Doctors wanted to pinpoint the exact variant or recessive gene that contributed to his cancer diagnosis. A brilliant female Mayo geneticist explained in lay terms that the results had shown a recessive TP53 gene that was most likely inherited from recessive genes in his birthparents. Unfortunately, this particular variant proves very challenging to rein in. She answered our questions and strongly encouraged Jeffrey to agree to an additional biopsy to determine whether this variant had been passed on to his son's DNA. He agreed and the next day, a large biopsy was done to find out. I don't know what the results showed, and I'm not sure I ever want to know.

By Christmas, Jeffrey's infections, platelet infusions, and blood transfusions seem to pick up in occurrence, causing more frequent hospitalizations. It was a very difficult thing for John and I to witness as parents. We were now often hands-on help in caring for Jeffrey's needs. Nothing seemed to be working to get him into remission, no matter how hard he tried. For the first time, I started caving into all the "what ifs" I never wanted to face.

After sitting for long stretches of time, my body would often scream at me to move. So, while Jeffrey was napping, I ventured on walks throughout the expansive hospital. Finally, after taking the elevator back up to seventh floor, I would often retreat to the family room to quickly check my cell phone before rejoining Jeffrey. On one of those visits, an attractive woman with a friendly smile and an all-too-familiar look of worry sat down across from me. Marla and I began conversing and soon divulged the reason that each of us now called Mayo our temporary "haven of hope". Both of us felt the importance of being on the floor early in morning for doctors' rounds, and it was common for our paths to cross. It was important to me that I was present for this daily interaction with doctors and provided me with important ways to support and understand my son's current medical status. Jeffrey was a man of few words and short answers. Like many times before, I functioned as a bridge to ask the necessary questions and share pertinent observations with his medical team. While caregiving for Jeffrey, I would typically be at the hospital from 8:00 in the morning after 9:00 at night. As amazing as medical staff at Mayo were, at times I was able to enhance his care because I was there with him.

Battling this aggressive disease zapped Jeffrey of so much energy. Always a finicky eater, he now had even less interest in eating. Yet he required good nutrition to maintain a healthy weight and to fuel his fight against a galloping disease. On those days he was with me at the GOL, I took him to his favorite Taco Johns for a taco fix or to Flapdoodles to get homemade ice cream. Daily, I would use the GOL kitchen to prepare his favorite home-cooked foods for breakfast, lunch, and dinner. When his home was the hospital, I would deliver many homemade meals to him there in hopes that he would be enticed into eating. When that wasn't successful, I found myself retrieving food from the hospital's Dairy Queen or the Chipotle across the street. Interesting him in food of any kind became my daily quest. It became a challenge to push up his calorie intake to slow the pace of his growing disease. It was anyone's guess as to how long anything he ate would stay in his system. Seeing that Jeffrey's caloric intake and his prescribed daily quota of protein drinks were downed were frustrating and challenging components of caretaking.

These were long, intense days. I strived hard to make them as positive and as comfortable as possible for Jeffrey. His nurses loved his non-demanding nature and his kind appreciation toward them. On nights when the kitchen was closed and his craving for ice cream kicked in, his doting nurses were all over it. Cleverly, Jeffrey mentioned his craving to a few nurses one at a time, and the scavenger hunt to secure their patient an ice cream bar became a secret competitive event. One by one, they would reappear to present Jeffrey with the golden prize, until he got busted when all three of them showed up with ice cream bars at the same time.

During my stays with Jeffrey, he taught me to slightly improve my jigsaw puzzle skills, and I soaked in time with him watching pro-basketball and baseball games. Sometimes, he would agree to let me watch "my shows", which were always news oriented. I felt the need to find out what was happening outside of our hospital cocoon. Due to being so absorbed the medical world, I felt uncomfortably out of touch with the bigger world around me. I was trying with everything in me to help save my boy and make him better, and I took it upon myself to help provide a change of scenery and some activities to rebuild his strength. We were able to reunite him with his laptop and gaming equipment to help pass time between appointments at the clinic and during hospitalizations. His self-installed gaming operation was close at hand and rigged to both his computer and hospital TV for instant entertainment. After seeing his gaming set up, one of his younger doctors promised a return visit to play Fortnight the following Saturday. It meant a lot to Jeffrey that he kept that promise.

His wife and little boy traveled to see him as often as his son's school schedule would allow. Because Jeffrey's physical status and need for infusions could fluctuate drastically from day to day, it was nearly impossible for them to make any firm plans. If blood draws showed that Jeffrey required blood transfusions or platelet infusions, it could take up half of the day with no guarantee as to how he would feel at the end. When his family came to visit, we attempted to be respectful of their precious time alone. It broke our hearts to see how much this ugly disease had stolen from them. I prayed that they would somehow be able to create some good family memories. We wanted nothing more than for them to be able to reunite again. Because of his wife and son, Jeffrey refused to stop fighting, knowing that the choice to stop was always his to make.

Elizabeth and Ondrea and some of Jeffrey's nieces and nephews made visits to see him at Mayo, which helped lift his spirits. Early in December, Jeffrey started spending more time in the hospital than the GOL House. He had a few serious side effect episodes that had everyone quite worried. But as before, he was able to make miraculous comebacks that amazed his doctors. Still, it was evident that Jeffrey was beginning to sleep more of the time. He seemed to be changing physically at a faster rate now that he had lost even more muscle mass and strength. I began to see changes in the look of his handsome face that stabbed me with reality. Because he was so sedentary, doctors recommended that Jeffrey take daily walks around the 7th floor. Sometimes, the hardest part was convincing him to put his shoes on his feet. Days were exhausting for him, and I became exhausted just watching him struggle. At my suggestion, he was prescribed a few physical therapy sessions and he had his resistance bands brought from home for follow-up workouts. In the long haul, these attempts were not sustainable. Earlier, a social worker rounded up a card table to keep in his room for jigsaw puzzles. The massage therapist came as often as Jeffrey's platelet levels would allow, to help his muscles relax. He even tried a couple of music therapy sessions.

The terms blast count, neutrophils, names for complex pulmonary or respiratory breathing treatments, and hard-to-pronounce oncological medications started to invade and take even more space and priority in Jeffrey's life. Medical doctors were constantly adjusting and readjusting chemo concoctions and medications to reverse his cancer, with the end goal of remission. And time after time, these efforts fell short. The clock was running out, and eventually Jeffrey's cancer morphed into a more serious form of leukemia, Acute Myeloid Leukemia or AML. This was a huge set-back in Jeffrey's prognosis. Infections, pneumonias, plate-lets, transfusions, scans, and routine bone marrow biopsies continued to comprise most of Jeffrey's days. His neutrophil, or white blood cell, levels were consistently low, making it nearly impossible for his immune system to fight off infections. As a result of having cancer, he made mask wearing popular several months before COVID-19 arrived. Low platelet levels prohibited clotting, and even scratches or small cuts could cause non-stop blood loss. Jeffrey's body was exhausted from jumping hurdle after hurdle with no progress. Staying strong and positive for him was the most challenging part of caretaking for me. I hated watching my once-strong boy being let down time after time and seeing him struggle relentlessly.

Jeffrey was getting antsy and frustrated with the lack of success he was seeing. After countless chemo trials, he felt locked in a time loop, same routine, different day, just like the movie "Groundhog Day". At about that point, John and I stepped up our caregiving in the hospital to give him additional comfort and help with nosebleeds, fevers, and vom-iting episodes.

On days when pain and worry started to strangle me from within, I would step outside the hospital room and head toward the big outside window with what my friend Marla and I called the "bench at the end of the hall". It made for a perfect perch to get a quick change of surround-ings. The best times on that bench were those shared with Marla. With a Styrofoam cup of coffee in hand, we vented our latest worries and tried our best to share a hug or a smile. No matter what dire happenings were occurring within the rooms of our loved ones, we knew we could find comfort in each other on our special bench. Located just out of earshot of the nurse's station and our loved ones, we still had full vision of the activity on the hospital wing. Meet-ups with Marla always made things better. I was sad to see her finally transport her husband back to their hometown in North Dakota for continued medical treatment. She had become an anchor in my out-of-control world. We have kept in touch, and I will always cherish her compassionate spirit and our time on the "bench at the end of the hall".

In early December, Jeffrey was placed on a new chemo that doctors were hoping would be a turn-around treatment in his cancer battle. He would receive this chemo concoction for fifteen days, after which he would have another bone marrow biopsy to access its success. We tried to stay on course and remain realistic about Jeffrey's chances. He seemed to feel invigorated and had no medical setbacks with the chemo. Despite his disdain for the hospital menu, Jeffrey's appetite seemed slightly improved. The day finally came for the tell-tale bone marrow biopsy. Now it was wait-time. The resulting number of blast cells remaining in his bone marrow would tell the truth of his prognosis. Jeffrey's oncology doctor was notified of the biopsy results as he deboarded the plane from India to Minneapolis. We were told he headed straight to the hospital to share them with Jeffrey. As he came into Jeffrey's room, his face told us first what his words would next. Jeffrey's post-chemo blood level results showed a disturbing and significant increase in the level of blasts which measured the amount of leukemia in his blood stream. This deflating news brought us to our knees. How could this be? Jeffrey had seemed to show signs of a rally after this latest chemo. We had shared a lot of unspoken hope that this treatment might be the step toward the remission we had hoped and prayed for. This fickle disease had already cruelly fooled us countless times, and now it had done it once more when it mattered the most. The doctor looked straight at Jeffrey and spoke in a soft serious voice. My heart sank when he reminded my son that he alone would decide whether his quest for treatment was over. I remember looking at the white tile floor unable to breathe as I reassured Jeffrey that it was absolutely and completely his decision. In seconds, Jeffrey said adamantly "Oh no! I'm not giving up!" This was my signal to cautiously breathe again.

That is when we learned of a possible last-chance option at the University of Texas MD Anderson Cancer Center in Houston, a global leader in cancer care, research, education, and training. With Jeffrey's permission, the doctor agreed to plead Jeffrey's case with a doctor he knew there, to see if there were any current research studies or treatments that might be a fit.

It was a few days later, but a big hallelujah when MD Anderson accepted Jeffrey as a part of an upcoming clinical trial. Plans were immediately made for Jeff to leave Mayo and travel to Houston with his wife. The morning they were to leave for the airport, Minnesota winter weather hit hard. It took a miracle and lots of problem solving, but they made it to the airport in time for their flight. Jeffrey got safely settled into the hospital by the grace of God and his wife. John would fly out to Houston so his wife could come back to work and care for their son.

I joined Jeffrey two weeks after Christmas, and we resumed our rotating care schedule. I got set up in living quarters with a kitchenette at a nearby hotel within walking distance of MD Anderson. John caught his flight to return home, while I acclimated myself to my new surroundings.

I was in awe of this huge medical complex, by the kindness of its people, and by a refreshed sense of hope that the medical staff made sure we felt. I was so grateful for Jeffrey's new chance at remission. At this hospital, if one option failed, we could be assured that another study would follow. A huge volume of clinical cancer trials and treatments originate from the Texas Medical Center. One entire hospital is solely filled with cancer patients, each one praying and pleading for one more chance to defeat this cruel disease. The World of the Sick was even more evident at MD Anderson.

The hospital shuttle provided by the hotel had one particularly upbeat driver who loved to lift our worried minds and spirits through song, along with hopes of a deposit in his tip jar. I quickly memorized the stops and realized that Houston's people are considerably nicer than the condition of their roadways. Rides on the shuttle were bumpy and wild, yet thankfully short. The hotel shuttle also scheduled drop-off and pickup services to a nearby Super Target. This allowed me to keep a few groceries on hand, enabling me to take food up to the hospital. Jeffrey's reduced appetite followed him to Houston. I tried to deny the growing look of weariness and discouragement in Jeffrey's eyes. It frightened me, and I wanted to make it go away. Yet he continued to rally after every scary drug reaction, infection, blood transfusion, bag of platelets, and discouraging blood report. His resolve and commitment to defeat his disease was simply incredible. Jeffrey would not quit, and as long as he struggled to win, I would be there cheering him on. However, as trial after trial did not produce the improvement that he so badly needed, the lights of hope began to flicker.

At MD Anderson, I met more people who became hope holders for me. Karen was one of them. We kept seeing each other on random visits to the cafeteria and would exchange smiles. One day, I asked if I could sit with her at her table. She said yes, and from then on, we shared our sagas whenever our paths crossed.

Jeffrey and I were watching TV one evening when I was approached by a floor nurse who blessed me with an unexpected opportunity. I was asked if I would consider assuming the role of "hope holder" for a complete stranger who was a patient down the hall. I agreed to become one of two needed witnesses for a middle-aged woman in her end stages of cancer. This fragile lady had been waiting for the moment when she was finally strong enough to sign with an X on a legal document that would allow her not to be resuscitated. The nurse seemed to support her patient into seizing this moment to legalize her healthcare wishes. The woman had no family or friends at her side in this moment of need. As a result of her cancer, she could no longer verbalize, but I will never forget how she spoke with her eyes as she looked at me. I felt a clear message of thankfulness and appreciation for agreeing to help make her final desires come true. It was one of the most reverent and sacred moments of my life. I was extremely touched and humbled and gave her my wish for God's love and peace as I turned to leave the room. It was a privilege to hold hope for a profound moment in this stranger's life. Similar to Mayo, the faces I passed in the hospital corridors and while riding the elevators told wordless stories of concern and sadness.

Sometimes my eyes locked with someone's, and a long informative chat might magically ensue. Such was the case with Erica. This attractive single mother seemed the model of a devoted caregiver whose mother was also battling leukemia on the same floor as Jeffrey. Erica stayed on top of every detail of her mother's medical care. I believe we were drawn together for the purpose of sharing support. Erica and I shared the same unlimited energy and devotion in leaving no stone unturned when it came to the care and treatment of our loved ones. Erica enthusiastically described an incredible place that she and her family were staying called the Halo House. This facility provided short-term, reduced-rate accommodations to caretakers and patients receiving active treatment at MD Anderson for different types of blood cancers. It sounded so amazing, and Erica urged me to give them a call and get on the waiting list. Erica then shared with the director of Halo House our situation of staying in a costly hotel while our son was hospitalized. I'm sure that conversation made all the difference, because within a couple of days I received a call saying they had an available apartment.

At that point, I began to realize that our time at MD Anderson would likely not be long. The next day, I packed our food and clothes and checked out of the hotel. Feeling like a vagabond, I ubered my way to move into Halo House several miles away. As soon as I walked through the front doors, I immediately felt at home. Erica was not wrong. Halo House was everything she had described and more. How refreshing it would be leaving the hospital and its barren environment, beeping machines, and dinging bells at the end of the day to retreat to this beautiful place that offered solace and a peaceful reset. My temporary oasis brought me comfort in a nurturing way that hotel life just couldn't. Watching Jeffrey's body being ravaged by disease was really taking a toll, and the quiet beauty of Halo House helped me stay afloat. The apartment possessed just the right amount of beauty and asylum to restore some of what Jeffrey's cancer had stolen from me. Perhaps this is why God gifts us with aesthetic beauty, to provide order and help us survive the bleak and dreary times.

One of my favorite escapes from the hospital was to go outside for "Flower Power" walks. Inhaling the beauty of the flowers temporarily revived me enough to walk back through the hospital doors where the marble walls seem to echo worry and concern. Another favorite distraction was to walk through the gift shop to sniff and sample the different fragrances of goat lotion sold there. Then, I might fetch a cup of freshly brewed Starbucks coffee before heading back up the elevator to 7th floor.

My new digs also provided a shuttle service that delivered me to the hospital early in the morning and back to the Halo House late at night. Our entertaining female shuttle driver had extra-long acrylic nails, thick false eyelashes, and a heavy southern drawl that she used while bantering with riders. I craved humor, and this provided me with a novel distraction from the impending seriousness every new morning brought.

In early February 2020, Jeffrey developed issues with high blood sugar, a side effect of medications. With little to no new improvement in my son's cancer status, my heart started closing doors to the alarming thoughts my mind was sending it. I was quickly becoming a "stand-alone" who was not only standing alone, but lonely. It seemed my courageous boy was trapped in a tsunami, with one forceful wave after another slamming him down. I told myself that this disease was now bigger than all the brilliant professionals and my overpowering longing as a mom to see him well. My mind was continuously sending me frightening glimpses of what lay ahead, and I challenged myself to stay with the intrusive images and stare them down in hopes they'd move on. My heart felt like it was being ripped from my chest, and the deep sadness of watching my handsome, once-healthy son wither away into a skeleton before my eyes paralyzed me. But one thing death could never rob Jeffrey of was his beautiful soul that knew how much he was loved. If he had to leave, he would leave knowing the most important thing.

I will never forget the day that doctors came to share the daunting results of his last trial and to tell him that MD Anderson could do no more to save my son's life. I left the room to give Jeffrey privacy for a conference call with the doctors and his wife. I barely made it out of the room before melting into a heap of tears on the hallway floor. All these months of praying, hoping, and exhaustion had finally taken me down. A nurse coming down the hallway corridor asked if I needed help or would like to talk to a clergy member or a social worker. "No", I mouthed. Somehow, I made it down the long hallway and collapsed on a couch in a vacant darkened family room. Rolled up in a tight ball to shut out the light and the world around me, I sobbed myself into oblivion. When I gathered enough strength, I realized that I needed to be with my son when he needed his mother most. I dreaded to see the disappointment on his face, but I would not abandon Jeffrey now. I could sense that the lights of hope now went from a flickering to an undeniable dimming.

Jeffrey had finished his conversation with his wife, and the doctors were gone. As I entered through the heavy doors of my son's room, I could see my sad and disappointed son. He looked let down, but strangely not broken by the punch he had just been delivered. He and his wife had called an end to the fight. The crazy roller coaster ride we had all been on for so long was going to stop. There would be no gearing up for another round of disappointment. I gently put my arms around him, and I can't remember exactly what was said. It was so much to process for each of us. Sitting back in the chair next to his bed, we sat in silence. Then I reached out my hand, and he held it for a long time. I promised him again that we would be with him for the rest of his journey. Our beautiful grandson would always be part of our life and family. Nothing could stop us from staying connected, as he was a part of Jeffrey and a part of us.

"Be sure Dad teaches him how to shoot a basketball right," Jeffrey said. For a moment, I could sense that Jeffrey had taken a slight bend toward the road of acceptance. I also should not have been surprised that my son's logical mind was already at work making a plan to get home. He had said adamantly and often that he did not want to die in Houston away from his family. For the first time, I didn't try to convince him that hope could be hiding right around the corner. Time wasn't on our side, and there were plans to be made. His dad had promised Jeffrey from the very beginning that no matter where his treatment took him or what the outcome, he would bring Jeffrey home. It felt like our hearts were dying but we were resolved to make that happen.

Jeffrey had an unexpected string of five good days, unusual considering this stage of his disease. He would not be discharged from the hospital unless he was strong enough to make the transfer. We knew his window of opportunity for travel was narrow and could change on a dime. Four of his days were spent waiting as his wife steadfastly researched and advocated for options to get Jeffrey back to Sanford Hospital for his final days. Their insurance company continued to reject coverage for air ambulance of any type. After four tense days of wrangling, they finally agreed to cover a ground ambulance from Houston to Fargo. Now, everything needed to move fast and without complications.

John flew into Houston the next day to fulfill his promise to his son. The doctors and nurses helped make this transfer as seamless as possible. After all the necessary paperwork had been completed and a ground ambulance team found, Jeffrey was set to make his journey home. John spent the night on the couch with Jeffrey, and I said my goodbyes just in time to catch the last shuttle back to Halo House. A storm of emotions passed through me as I cleaned out the apartment at Halo House and got everything packed for my flight home to Fargo the next day. I prayed hard for our medically fragile son to be stable enough when the sun came up to make the trip.

By the grace of God and Jeffrey's strong will, all went as planned. With John sitting on the hard bench seat next to his boy's side, their grueling non-stop 24-hour ambulance journey began. Jeffrey tolerated it as well as could be expected. He knew that every mile traveled brought him closer to home. His wife and son were anxiously waiting, knowing it would be early the next morning before the ground ambulance carrying their precious cargo would arrive. Everything was ready on Sanford's end.

Once I reached Fargo and arrived back home at the lake, I inhaled the comfort of being home again. I went to sleep with my cell phone, waiting for the call from John saying they had safely arrived at Sanford. My head was spinning with all that had transpired in the last hours. About 4:00 in the morning the call came. They had safely made it back home. I was relieved and happy that Jeffrey got his wish.

John had an extremely close bond with our son Jeffrey, and I am sure his dad's presence and calm brought him unbelievable comfort and peace on the long journey. Throughout this entire homecoming process, I fell deeply in love with my husband all over again. I saw once more how very much John loved his son and how he was always there to wrap his amazing father's love around him and every one of his children when they needed him.

Our window of time with Jeffrey was narrowing. We could never be ready for the end that was coming. The doctor's plan for Jeffrey was to keep him on the oncology floor as long as he was medically stable. Then he would move to the hospice floor. It was during his time on the oncology floor that so much magic happened. John and I were there every day, and were shocked to immediately observe that where there had once been multiple bags and monitors attached to an IV pole, there were now only two bags. It was relieving and unsettling at the same time. Jeffrey's health journey had been given back to him in whole. Now, each time I glanced at his wrist, I saw the brashly printed letters DNR. I wondered how Jeffrey felt looking at that, as my own feelings couldn't be put into words.

He had strong support from family and friends, and he was able to spend time with his little boy who loved to sit in his hospital bed with his daddy and play computer games. From a social standpoint, we had no idea of the number of friends that wanted to spend time with Jeffrey in his first week back. It was heartwarming to see the eclectic group of people who came together as one with him in his last days in an attempt to capture all the time they could with him. It was a living example of his ability to be non-judgmental and accepting of people. We were surprised by the number of friends who each had a valued connection with Jeffrey. I was so reaffirmed as his mother to see that the authentic beauty and light of Jeffrey had been recognized by others after all. I recognized the impact my quietly powerful son had made on so many lives, and I was grateful.

Seeing and hearing from those present seemed to nourish Jeffrey's soul with a glow and contentment that I had never seen in him before. He was sitting up in his bed beaming with his beautiful smile enjoying every moment. He was the star of the show, and for once he enjoyed being the center of attention. Hearing meaningful and humorous memories that were wrapped in laughter was such a gift to Jeffrey and to all of us who loved him. At the end, life really boils down to memories and relationships made through human connection and unconditional love. The struggles of life are no longer complex and our path toward transition is shown in the clearest light, calling us on with assurance and peace. Jeffrey's unbelievable acceptance helped me further accept his entry into the Hospice unit where I was caught up in the peace of Jeffrey's spiritual release into another dimension.

Before he entered hospice, he asked me to write his obituary. Even though I never thought I would be called on to write two obituaries in five years for my own children, I agreed. That night my thoughts flowed onto paper. I was finding the strength to do so many hard and challenging things I'd never been called to do before. The grace of divine courage was carrying me through. Jeffrey had learned so much from sports and about the game of life itself. The important thing is to show up, to try your hardest, and to accept that both wins and losses as a part of the game. Baseball was his all-time passion. Knowing this, I concluded his obituary with "All your family and friends have been cheering you on. Congratulations! You have just hit the biggest home run of your entire life! Welcome Home, Jeffrey."

Watching my son read his obituary made me feel like I had hit a homerun as well. When he finished, he looked up with tears in his eyes and said quietly and humbly, "Thanks, Mom." I only hope he knew that there were no words amazing enough to describe his beautiful self. It was my absolute joy to have him as my son. Nevertheless, writing his obituary and allowing him to read it was hard for this mom to process. Reality was setting in deeper, and I didn't like how it unsettled every cell of my body. How was I supposed to be ready to lose him? The air around me felt heavy with urgency.

A couple of days after he entered the Hospice unit, he was moved to a room closer to the nurse's station. Jeffrey's wife, who was staying overnight with him, was sitting near the head of his bed and Jeffrey was markedly weaker. The change in him was so startling that I stepped back into the hallway and lost it. I realized I was not prepared to see my child's body and soul begin to separate. It wouldn't be long now. He remained in a semi-conscious state, enveloped by our continual words of love and affirmation and his favorite quiet and calming music, the "good music". The nurse lowered the side rail of his bed so I could put my face next to his on his pillow. I told him over and over again as I lightly touched his arm and face to not be afraid, that he was so loved by me, and that I would be there for him always. My husband had quieter presence with him, but rarely left his side. Within his room, I sensed an awareness that is hard to explain with words. A feeling of peaceful sacredness dominated the room. I found myself wishing that he would move forward in his journey and that his soul was readying itself for departure into something better in the beyond. I never thought I'd say that I wanted that for him now. He deserved to be free again.

John and I left the room during the day occasionally to give each other quiet moments alone with Jeffrey. Rarely if ever did Jeffrey open his eyes. Once when we were alone, he turned his head toward my face and peered straight into my eyes. I smiled back at him for these precious couple of minutes as he continued to stare at me. I wanted him to leave seeing my love shine. I got the distinct message that he was telling me how thankful he was and how much he loved having me as his mom. All I could do was smile back and gaze into his eyes as this moment of love sealed itself into my heart forever.

On another occasion while we were alone, I felt the presence of others who had gone ahead. I really feel that Jeffrey did too. Once as I stepped back into the room after retrieving a cup of coffee, he turned his face to the side with the most beautiful smile on his face, as if someone was there to guide him home. Just from the way he smiled, I sensed it could have been his brother Joshua who could often take him by surprise with his humorous comments. Seeing one of his last earthly smiles brought me peace and the hope that he would soon find eternal happiness. I will be forever grateful for that simple treasured smile. That afternoon, Jeffrey's son was brought up for a final visit. I began to wonder if that is what was holding Jeffrey back from allowing God to take him. The visit by his boy was short but appeared to be a real change maker.

When his wife returned a few hours later, we got ready to go home. We were glad that Jeffrey's wife would stay with him through the night. Before we left, I looked at him and said, "We'll see you tomorrow, or we'll see you in heaven if you decide to leave tonight. Dad and I will not be far behind. I love you." It was a hard ride home.

John was outside with our dogs before we left for the hospital on March 5, 2020, when Jeffrey's wife called. He came through the back door, threw the dog leashes to the floor and cried out, "He's gone!" Jeffrey had left this world peacefully, holding his wife's hand. He had finally transitioned into a place of wholeness. His journey was done. My initial reaction was a mixture of sadness and relief. What we could never be fully prepared for was the lasting finality of his absence. We drove in silence to the hospital. I was numb and teary as I closed my eyes to gather enough strength from the universe to say what would be one of my many goodbyes to my third son.

Jeffrey had a beautiful memorial service lovingly shaped by his wife. She did a touching job with picture boards and floral displays cleverly arranged around selected pieces of Jeffrey's favorite sports memorabilia.

His medals, hockey stick, and special red Darrel Strawberry baseball glove were almost too difficult for me to look at, even adorned by flowers. Each of those who joined us to celebrate of our son's precious life provided more support than they could ever realize.

Anyone who really knew Jeffrey knew he loved tacos. Eating tacos by Jeffrey's request at his funeral reception was a wonderful way to honor his true essence. While visiting the cemetery that day, it broke our hearts to see Jeffrey's overwhelmed little boy bending over his daddy's grave to say goodbye. When I turned around to leave, I found myself falling into the arms of my sister, who was there to save me once again. John and I were nearly lifeless ourselves as we returned with family members to our safe place, our peaceful home, our sacred retreat on the lake.

Just one day after Jeffrey's funeral, the world began shutting its doors as a protection against the spread of COVID-19. People cocooned inside in order to escape the deadly illness for which no protection was available. People like me in the grip of grief could find some small solace in these circumstances. It wasn't as if the world was flying by and leaving us behind. Everyone's world had in some way come to a halt. By the end of the pandemic, after the deaths of over a million people in our country and the illness of many more, our world would have been veiled by a type of collective grief.

By nature, I am a hugger and a people person. Fortunately, I could survive for a while on all the hugs and words of comfort that I received after Jeffrey's death. Those of us who lost loved ones during the pandemic had our grief doubled. Not only were our loved ones gone, but the world had left us isolated too! I was in a very desperate place, trying to make sense out of Jeffrey's loss when there was none to be found. I felt irreparably broken, and I was blinded to seeing any possible way out of the resulting pain. The huge sense of disconnection and isolation that I felt was crippling with the death of Jeffrey and the pandemic. In Jeffrey's final days, I found reprieve by putting my feelings on paper in the hopes of releasing a small portion of overwhelming hopelessness.

Free Falling

April 2020

I'm free falling again. I've been thrust into this same dark place before. I wasn't invited and don't want to be here, but fate will have its way and hold me here yet again. I feel totally powerless and devoid of energy. The familiarity of what lies ahead of me steals my peace but yet has shown me that I will have a fighting chance of survival. I have somehow survived before. It is dire, frightening, exhausting and sorrowful, this pit of grief into which I've been cast. How do I look at this beautiful grown child of mine, breathe in the reality of his morbid diagnosis, and exhale without screaming? Where is the book that tells me how to guide my child through his death? Where is the magic formula that will provide me the words to give comfort to my logical son? How is it possible for a mother to comfort her son who is confronting his own mortality at the age of 39? Where is the fairness in this? Where is the person to lean on, who knows this journey and has walked it? Who will take my shaking hand and lead me forward to the light as I walk my child Home?

Walking this journey with my son will be the most difficult and heart-wrenching act of love I will ever be called upon to fulfill as a parent. It will require inconceivable courage and commitment. While I watch my boy dying from the inside out, I will be dying along with him from the outside in. I am obligated to do right by my son. I can't screw this up, as there won't be a do-over. I will need to make all the correct turns at the right time and with perfect pilot vision. I must carefully choose words that will bring him comfort and peace and will assuage the fear in him and in me. I need to move into his shadow so that I feel one with him, while seeing ahead of him to anticipate his needs and wants long after his voice goes. And one more time, the most prized of all life's blessings will be snatched from my life to vanish from this world, never to be seen or felt by me again. I desperately call out Jeffrey's name over and over, until it fades to a whisper, and my swollen eyes have mercifully closed to make it all seem like a bad dream. As I lay there broken held by the pillows that cradle my throbbing head, my heart feels splayed open and vulnerable. My body goes limp, and I feel unable to move in any direction. I am only breathing out of habit. And the question screams at me, "What mother would ever think it possible to help journey their own child into the afterlife?" After all, mother minds are focused on bringing new life into this world, not sending that life on to another realm. A dying child's mother holds that precious life in safety and, while holding them close, expels them away into the unknown. When they are babies, mothers breathe love into their cherished and beautiful little souls, praying that by God's grace they will blossom beyond our dreams. Our blindly naïve mother minds are not designed to recognize the unfathomable concept of child loss. As a parent, we understand that life is linear. Our universal belief is that a child's life stretches out far beyond our lifetime as parents. My belief about the innate goodness of the universe is challenged now. Surely life does not disperse these treasured children into the earth and loving families only to cruelly allow their journeys here to be shortened and cut short before our eyes? Losing a child is the ultimate extinguisher of dreams, and it temporarily removes a parent's desire or reason for existence.

Meanwhile, I lie in my trauma. It became crystal clear to me that the truth is that I am about to mother another of my three precious boys through his life and into death. Did I have the strength to clamor my way up out of this abhorrent pit of despair for the third time? I will need my entire body to find its way up to be there for my son. Like a lotus, I will need to rise through the thick viscous mud and travel upward to a point of clarity and light to be there for my son. It will require a vast and draining amount of strength and focus. Will I be there for the loving send-off Jeffrey so deserves? Waiting for someone to rescue me, I subconsciously remind myself that no one can make the fact of my child's death magically go away. I am forced to make a choice that will change me no matter what I decide. Somewhere, buried deep down inside my heart, I sense an inaudible answer that nudges me. Once again, I will do the most unthinkable task.. and I will survive.

Losing one child is inexplicably difficult, two children lost is horrific, but three children is a loss beyond description. I am broken, and there is no easy way out of this pain. It is all encompassing and wraps me like struggling prey in a boa's constricting hold. I am fighting to breathe, and I frantically grab onto the flapping coattails of life.

With relief, I am released by the hold of my captor. I sputter and ground myself, as I become aware that invisible inner forces have al-

ready decided my fate. Recapturing my determination, I will climb up and out, and I will say yes. I will be strong and ready myself to share the soothing waters of my mother well with my dying son. This journey through hell and back will take every bit of human might and energy I can muster. I have done this twice before, but each journey is so different. Despising this ominous state of deja vu, I imagine a bomb detonating in my heart, shattering all but the ticking which is the last thread connecting me to life. It is my beating heart that screams back to me with desperate love and promises to provide a lifeline between my boy and me. But, all my eyes can envision now is a 1000-piece puzzle strewn helter-skelter and floating in space. This puzzle is much too complicated and overwhelming for me to piece together. I notice the darkness of my colors. Internally, I imagine I am bluish black in places where my heart has been destroyed and has lost its vibrant color. Mine is a picture of a soul that is weak and badly beaten. Where do I even begin? Unmercifully, my mind keeps taking me back there again and again, forcing me to see something. What did I miss before in this sad wreckage of despair?

And then staring, miraculously, I began to see a subtle flicker, small and hidden but still emitting light. My eyes began to focus on it as I realize it to be my light of hope and possibility, hidden in the rubble all along. What a miracle that this flicker continues to survive deep within me. At first, this dim but firm light is a blur, difficult to see through the murky and heavy aftermath of disaster in my heart. My eyes grab onto this barely recognizable flicker and I see that the more I hold it, the stronger my hope light grows. I am gently pulled up off the ground to begin this rugged journey by the only source of strength I can unconditionally trust, my rock, my God.

Feeling the need to remind myself to breathe, I whisper over and over a verse from Philippians 4:13: "I can do all things through Christ who strengthens me". And so begins the climb, as I cling with white knuckles to the barely visible light of the lantern, my only source of light through the dark foreboding world of death.

I make my way up through the muck and misery refusing to allow my thoughts to drift backwards to what was. Instead, my mind is set in perpetual and forward motion. And so begins my next journey toward acceptance.

Epilogue

And once the storm is over you won't remember how you made it through, how you managed to survive. You won't even be sure, whether the storm is really over. But one thing is certain. When you come out of the storm you won't be the same person who walked in.

Haruki Murakami

When a loved one dies, a grief dance occurs. Grief makes every attempt to steal the lead on the dance floor of life. Ironically, grief requires dominance in order to transform our out-of-control grief into a form of sweet sorrow. In grief's arms, we are swooped in and out of the reality of death's finality like a rag doll, until we reluctantly surrender to the concept of acceptance. The journey of grief is not really about our loved one who has already transitioned and is at peace. It is about the griever and the winding journey toward the acceptance of living without the physical presence of their loved one. Our grief is also not about our spouse, or children, or grandchildren. They are deserving of their own journey, with all their feelings, needs, and perspectives.

One day after Jeffrey's funeral on March 10, 2020, our country officially was shut down by the pandemic. For me, the isolation was an opportunity for deep introspection that was vitally important in working through the muck of my grief. I had to put on my heavy puddle boots, and splash right through the dirty water of sorrow. Sometimes the boots proved useless, and the water of grief washed over top of them. I learned in time to work my way along the edges when the water grew deeper, until I could feel my puddle boots touch the ground again. My intent was laser focused. This time, my journey back to the surface of life was more difficult and labor intensive than any I had traveled before.

The COVID-19 pandemic also provided this once outgoing and active woman a respite from the interaction and distraction of others. I had just experienced the bombing and implosion of my soul. All roads leading out and away from the scene of the accident appeared closed. Even though I felt trapped and isolated, I turned away from anyone who wanted to advise me through my sadness. I knew the toll it was taking on me. Sorrow and grieving left me no reserves. I had no energy and needed to descend deep within myself to protect my healing space from invasion. I needed to be alone with me. Fortunately, visitors were almost non-existent, and John screened my calls, as I seldom wanted to talk to anyone.

When my thoughts and internal chatter overwhelmed me, my body would dial me down and demand escape through rest. It was difficult for me to converse with my husband, daughters, and sister who were all there waiting to reach out. Everyone in our family was on their own heavy journey after Jeffrey's death, and going within myself offered me the only chance I had of self-survival. Thankfully, my wonderfully supportive husband understood this and helped me surround and preserve this necessary and sacred space by allowing me the isolation I needed.

Words were only noise to me, and the well-meaning words of people burdened me with new expectations that were neither within my sight nor capability. Advice only felt intrusive and heavy, pulling me further into myself. For the most part, well-meaning thoughts of others cluttered my heart and felt oppressive.

Around this same time, I began to experience reality breaks showing me the abhorrent truth of my loss. They ravaged my mind like a horror movie on rewind and made me cringe. Wanting to curl up and turn my back on life forever, I isolated myself inside my soundproof cocoon.

There I could hit the pause button and inhale again, until a cloud of exhaustion allowed me to retreat into shutdown mode.

I dreaded sleep. The hardest part was waking up and realizing the horrendous truth had never left my side. Once awake, the flood of tormenting thoughts and memories unmercifully resumed. I tried to stop the racing panic building inside, but I couldn't. This brutal and raw pain was relentless, and I had no control over its cruelty as it continued to run rampant and wild inside my mind. Occasionally, I felt an actual aching in my heart. When this would happen, I would instinctively cradle my heart in my cold hands while applying light pressure. Doing this seemed to diminish the ache just long enough to allow my deep guttural sobs to pour out directly from my heart. Where was the hope?

Losing a child is simply too much to take in, too much to try to fix, and too much human loss. I began to realize that my body miraculously allowed only as much emotional pain as my mind could process at any one point in time. This automatic regulation of pain was the very thing that kept me from going over the edge and losing all connection with the rational world. Perhaps this offered me the hope that I was so desperately trying to find.

If only there had been a five-step method that could have brought me to some understanding and glimmer of peaceful acceptance. If only there had been a guarantee that my world would heal again, and that I could once more feel inspiration and courage. If only I could have counted on the eventual return of purpose and joy in my life. Yet this tangled ball of sadness and grief intertwined with all its uncertainty, forming a knot that grew tighter by the minute. Grief threw me into a vulnerable place where I doubted the ability to ever reconnect to the beat of life. For now, all I could do was feed off the rhythm of others.

This third trip through child loss had put me in stranglehold. I suspect that having helplessly watched our medically fragile infant son die before my eyes significantly magnified the torment of final separation this time. The decision to release the string that connects a parent to their child forever is one no parent should have to make. Lonely despair locks a parent of child loss in a state of terror. I had to keep reminding my perfectionistic self that there is no recipe or magical way to recover from loss and no right or wrong way to grieve. Thankfully, this paralyzing kind of fear is not forever. I am here to share with you that there IS a choice before you to find the hope that now seems forever hidden.

For weeks and weeks, my mental and physical energy varied greatly from day to day. Spending concentrated time with myself while the pandemic shut me off from the usual pressures felt comfortable. In this space I could make plans to reboot my life. I began to think about the people who had been important to me, those I had missed seeing during our shutdown world. Ever since making the lake our permanent home, I have been a member of our community workout center. Here I have built a supportive network of multi-age women who are committed to staying fit and also share a love of coffee and dialogue. When Jeffrey's cancer was diagnosed, these "Wonder Women" stepped up to encourage and keep me afloat through the stressful months that followed. Unfortunately, the shutdown brought an abrupt end to these daily interactions that gave me so much support.

Taking care of my body through exercise and good nutrition had always been important to me. My breast cancer diagnosis had shown me how accumulated stress can ravage a body. Because the gym was now closed, I took to my feet outside. Emotionally, getting out of bed was hard, but by the end of summer 2020 I was walking a four-mile trek six days a week. When the Minnesota snow and cold weather returned, I kept my routine and enjoyed winter walks out in the cold, crisp air. In the quiet of nature, I sensed a lift in my mood and a spark of energy for the first time in months. Walking gave me a reason to get out of bed in the morning. About this time, I came across a couple of female comedian vloggers on Facebook. Listening to their vlogs while walking through the snowy woods and trails was another reason to enjoy my morning walk. Each of these middle-aged comedians joined the rest of the world on the struggle bus plugging through the pandemic's isolation and the resulting frustrations. Their relatable humor made everything more bearable. One memorable morning, a vlogger said something that made me double over in laughter. She will never know how indebted I am to her for helping me find my laugh again. It was a huge moment that moved me forward.

My attention span was zapped, but I tried to read and listen to as many grief books as I could. A pivotal experience occurred when I joined a nationally formed online grief support group, formed for those grieving alone during COVID. Participating five days a week in Zoom sessions led by national grief expert David Kessler taught me much about grief and loss and profoundly impacted me. I would venture to say that it played a major role in my survival. Coming together to learn and express our common feelings and concerns in grief was a powerful saving grace for me. I needed the grounding of routine in my days, and this provided me with one more consistent activity. The anonymity of virtual human connection and the opportunity to be seen and heard as I told my stories of child loss played a vital part in preserving my fragile mental health.

I also took advantage of many internet webinars and streamed conferences on the topic of grief and loss. Some were more beneficial than others, but all challenged my mind and opened it to new ideas and understanding. They kept my brain active and engaged in the grief process.

The pandemic gave everyone the equal opportunity to re-evaluate friendships and social circles. I felt the need to scrutinize my friendships and start fresh from the ground up. Who could I trust enough to allow into my small circle of support?

Child loss with all its morbidity is too frightening and intimidating for some people to wrap their heads around. Although it is not a catchy disease, they run away from this unthinkable fear instead of running toward those hurting and in need. It becomes more about what they can and can't handle or what they might say to the mourner. But we who are hurting from our loss know that simply the presence of support means everything. There are no "right words" that can change what happened. Sadly, what is lost when people walk away is the opportunity for expressing human compassion.

I needed a fresh start to match my new perspective. Being a giver and an encourager by nature, I saw that I had gathered people into my life who needed me, but seldom gave back. In my experience, friendships have typically shifted with each child loss. While some have stayed in my friendship circle, others who I thought I knew well chose to create distance. Their responses caught me by surprised and created a lot of hurt.

I accepted that some of these relationships needed to be set free without negative judgment. The entering and leaving of relationships is all part of the natural ebb and flow of friendship.

Fortunately, other friends who never walked away were waiting patiently on the sidelines with open arms, ready and waiting to support me. With their gifts of open acceptance, they welcomed this slightly re-arranged version of who I used to be. These special friends demonstrate what true friendship really is. Using them as a gold standard, I gathered the clarity to release and let go of people who no longer served my best interest. It was no longer about the quantity of friends but the quality of the people that I welcome into my life. It was time to direct love toward myself and to concentrate on reopening myself to the vulnerability of life and change.

My spirituality is the provider of continued connection with those I have lost through death. Their dying has changed me spiritually, and I am tremendously more "soul conscious" now. I am convinced that each of our souls arrives on earth with a very clear purpose and path. Some-times that purpose is very different from the one we believe to be ours. We unknowingly struggle to learn the true path of our souls through lov-ing and connection with others throughout our lives. Could it be that the child that has died has entered this world with a "soul contract" that was chosen in part by them and their creator? Perhaps we all arrive where, when, and with whom we do to fulfill our soul's predetermined purpose here on earth.

Even though there is never a right time for a child's soul to be ripped away from us, the soul has a different sense of timing, and leaves when it is time to go. Science tells us that people live and die with energy and that energy's inertia is ongoing and never stops existing. I have had communications with the souls of my boys that convince me of their constant presence in a realm just outside of ours. I have so much more to share with the children that I have lost, and find comfort in believing that I can continue a connection with each one at the soul level. Looking at my boys' lives through the lens of soul contracts, I can be nothing but proud and honored that they chose me to be their mom and to be one with our family. My children live on in me through leaving their unique gifts with me on earth: from John Ryan, courage; from Joshua, resilience; and from Jeffrey, acceptance. Their beautiful presence and souls' purposes have changed my perspective on living, dying, and on my very own soul's contract. I feel like I get it now. From this perspective, I can see the purpose of each of my boy's lives and deaths with much more clarity and understanding.

I became intrigued and open to enrolling in a few online writing classes. I created a writing office in a spare bedroom and put pen to paper. It didn't take long for me to see that creativity was a game changer in feeding my parched spirit.

My thoughts began seriously tilting toward the creation of this book. Only in the last quarter of my life have I realized that my passion to write a book about child loss is my soul contract, the purpose of my being that I have been searching for. The seed was planted and this book began to take shape in the back of my mind. I would make it happen.

Slowly, my attention span lengthened. I was holding weekly Zoom meetings with my therapist, who encouraged me to participate in meditation and other mindful activities. About this time, I discovered the Shift and the Commune Networks online and began signing up for various webinars that I thought would be helpful. One of the many that interested me was built around relaxation breathing. These helpful hour-long sessions gave me internal insight and vision and a way to regulate my breath into a state of relaxation and calm.

I also took up painting-by-number, working at my dining room table for 10 or 15-minute stretches several times throughout the day. The finished pictures were pretty enough to have framed and never fail to give me a feeling of self-satisfaction when I pass them on the walls of our home. They are a part of what brought me forward. To honor Jeffrey's attempt to make me a puzzle lover, I successfully completed a few 500-piece jigsaws—another mindful activity that proved to be a great distraction and challenge. Playing bridge was also welcomed back into my life. Since John and I could no longer meet with our contract Bridge group on Wednesday afternoons, we played several times a week as partners online.

A few months into lockdown, I realized how much I missed my beloved forever teacher friends. We have traveled the thick and thin times of life together, and have supported one another over the years. I was thrilled when we decided to resume our monthly book club over Zoom. Voila! Their beautiful faces appeared on screen right in front of me! Our Zoom reunion soon led to additional impromptu happy hours.

When our grief is raw, we are lucky if we can find another human who is open to listening and to witnessing our grief. Life has put such a person on my path after the death of each of our three sons. These "lamp holders" serve as angels in disguise during our time of grief and become guides to our re-entry into life. After John Ryan died, my friend Sandy was that lamp holder to whom I could tell and retell the details with all their rawness, and with no judgment or desire to "fix" my broken-ness. Sandy's open acceptance was a priceless gift to me. She was the bridge that led me over troubled waters, through the gift of her time and countless cups of coffee with Coffeemate. Though we have drifted apart geographically, I feel honored to have had her in my life and will remain grateful to her forever.

Mary was my lamp holder after Joshua died. Leave it to a dog to draw us together. Little did I know, during our first meeting on the bike path, what a dear friend she would become. She would also walk by my side through breast cancer, and Jeffrey's illness and death. Mary has helped lift me up through some of the darkest and deepest valleys of my life. And I met her on "the path".

My beloved husband and dearest friend could not take the place of my lamp holders. We were each too close sharing the common loss and grief of our children. John and I have had to learn that each of our jour-neys must be taken alone. Grief is solitary, and John and I have handled our grief very differently, with our own needs and perspectives, and at our own pace. The fact that we have made these solo journeys three times and are still together and happy after 54 years may well be because we were able to give each other the freedom of sacred and individual healing journeys with no judgment. I feel like our marriage has shifted and rearranged with each loss and continues to lay down new roots.

My wonderful friend Mary called me daily, even though her own life had been upended by her husband's health issues. When talking over the phone just didn't cut it, I would jump into my car and head across to the north shore of the lake. Here we may or may not have had a few for-bidden face-to-face happy hours in Mary's garage, with chairs arranged COVID-style, blankets, and a bottle of wine. These covert visits proved priceless every time.

I also began reconnecting via Zoom with my high school "potluck" group who have remained dear friends of mine since junior high school. We have experienced a lot of life's ups and downs together in the last 60 years. Our monthly meetings have reinforced connectivity and a special sisterhood that continues to feed and ground me today.

During this time, I was introduced to the healing world of *qi gong* and enrolled in two life-changing online courses taught by an instructor in Puerto Rico. *Qi gong* involves the use of body movements to move energy within the body, mind, and spirit, and helped me improve my overall well-being. Filling my days with meaningful learning and mind-ful doing was the key to helping me unlock doors to the closed world.

After losing Jeffrey and struggling through the health scare of COVID-19, time became more precious to me than ever. I noticed a sense of urgency in my daily life that helped nudge me toward new growth around grief. Each activity brought me sporadic moments of interaction which eventually coaxed me out of my isolation. I dared to look outward again. The door was routinely being cracked open ever so slightly, and the outside world began to shine small beams of light that beckoned me. Could this be the light of hope?

When I eventually ventured out masked, I saw that while other lives had gone on, mine had come to a full stop. People were moving again in their routines and responsibilities, and seemed oblivious to my loss. I had to remind myself this was because functioning humans had not been directly swallowed by the World of the Sick. They were living in a different paradigm. Watching others resume their former lives reassured me that life went on and that a world was waiting for me.

Still, I felt left behind. It bothered me that some were able to turn their faces forward and move on from the pandemic. I realized it was up to me to pick up the reins and steer out of the darkness and back on the road of the living. I am gifted with perseverance, and gently I began to turn my focus toward acceptance. As time moved me subtly forward, things started to appear a shade or two lighter around me. I inched my way further out of my isolation. Eventually, the outside world began to shine more hope and light. Once the door was fully opened, I was able to sense healing souls hovering right outside my door. They were each holding lamps that held the light of my hope for me while I could not. I began to see that my lamp holders had never left me, nor had my hope.

I felt encouraged by their presence, believing that at last I could trust myself to retell the true story of my loss, until I no longer felt the pressing need to do so. I was never broken. Instead, I was a mother mourning and in grief.

I continue to try to keep my trust circle small and to put out into the universe the expectation that I deserve to be treated with kindness and respect. In return, I try to do the same for others. Over the past few years, I have brought new and beautiful people into my life. I believe that I did not meet them by chance. These people are supposed to be with me, showing up at my weakest and bringing empathy, constancy, and hope back into my life. My hope holders have encouraged me to trust myself into full authenticity. Armed with empathy, these hope holders possess an understanding that grief is a process, not something that can be "snapped out of". These beautiful people freely give me the grace and understanding that I still need.

Like it or not, people who lose a child are forever changed by the experience. This loss has a way of humbling and molding people into humans who are clearly not here to please others, but to show a genuine version of their changed selves. Craving the wholesome goodness of people, I am now less tolerant of negativity. Reassessing my world has allowed me to protect the boundaries of my sacred inner-self, which deserves to be nurtured, loved, and held safe. If I guard and honor it, I will be gifted with an inextinguishable protective light. I have been determined not to let the loss of a third child take the whole of me with it. I am a lover of life and remain fervently committed to living out the remainder of my years with joy and peace. Through my decision to bring my three sons with me, John Ryan, Joshua, and Jeffrey are now able to continue to experience life through my eyes. I honor their beautiful souls by moving forward and keeping their memories alive in my heart. Showing up for myself and each of them requires me to muster up all the courage I can with each new day and expands me as a mother and a woman.

Embracing grief is difficult, but it has a lot to teach us. What we learn from grief can cause our self-growth to blossom and our lives to expand in unbelievable dimensions. Because of the loss of my boys, I am now more deeply compassionate and empathetic of others' losses.

After John Ryan died, I screamed with all certainty that I could never survive such loss again. And yet I did... two more times. Thus far in life, I have survived the desert of death and loss of three children, breast cancer, a global pandemic, and the loss of many other family members and friends. What could be left to fear?

To keep moving forward, I must remember that March 5, 2020, the day we lost Jeffrey, is over forever. I have experienced a thorough "self-cleaning" since Jeffrey's death. This purification has forced me to look at what now feeds me and aligns with what I want in human relationships and in deciding which beliefs are worth valuing and maintaining. There are things that once held importance that now have been discarded or moved down my list of priorities. In order to rebuild my heart, I have to put me and my reconstruction in first place. This process takes time, determination, and small baby steps to accomplish. This is the gift of grief.

I realize now that staying busy to avoid facing the raw discomfort of my thoughts has been my pattern in the past, and that it provides only a temporary lid over truths needing to be seen and processed. Underneath all the noise, staying in touch with my "knowing" is the only way I can stay divinely connected to myself and to my lost loved ones.

My mind can take an enormous pounding from what I tell myself. I have remained open to professional help to aid in diffusing feelings and shedding light on new perspectives. Grief counselors and personal therapists have been a lifeline. They have enabled me to create space where I can hold my thoughts and feelings and view them safely. They are mirrors that help me see things more clearly. Their suggestions have taught me how to reframe my thinking when I am stuck in the potholes of grief, allowing me to lift myself out and back on the road to restoration and acceptance.

In order to move through grief, it must be recognized and faced for what it is. There is no "healing" from loss, but it is possible to grow around it. It is my hope that something shared here encourages you and provides ideas to use in your own rebuilding after loss.

Most nights, I stare out my bedroom window at the sky over the lake and gaze at the moon and stars and the trees as they dance in the dark. To me, they offer a glimpse into eternity. In the summer, I see the beauty of dock lights shining on the lake as the waves rise and fall. White lights that illuminate the cross atop a cliff on the eastern shore promise me safety and comfort through each dark unknowing night. The lights, both outside on my pergola and in my flower garden, twinkle rhythmically with the stars, and together they create a nightlight that shines faith back into my doubting heart. I am reminded of how blessed I am and of my gift of faith that gets me through even the most desolate of times.

It is sometimes hard to fathom that just three years ago, Jeffrey led us through his illness, death, the pandemic, and returned us cautiously to rejoin the world as it is now. Still evolving and changing as a person in and out of grief, I miss each of my boys like crazy. I have written this book with the hope that others of you who are called to mediate this journey from a child's life into death will find comfort. I hope that you will recognize that the hope that seems to have vanished will follow the cycle of appearing, disappearing, and reappearing again in the fluid road of grief that leads toward acceptance. May you come to a place of knowing where you realize that death is only the recycling of our loved ones back to us into the loving safely of our hearts…never to leave us again. No matter the surrounding circumstances or the age of a child at the time of death, their dying takes a piece of the soul with it. It seems so difficult to believe that grief is part of our love for our child and is a healer and a friend. We are required to live while we grieve, and that is the most difficult challenge. I would give anything not to be this mother victimized by such cruel and consuming loss. I want to be free in my heart and have all my children with me as I grow old, like so many others I see around me.

May you feel my fervent desire to help parents who are walking this horrific path toward seemingly unobtainable acceptance. Because healing is not an option, grieving parents can only journey toward an acceptance that allows some peace and ability to live on. Honoring my boys and probing memories that were painful to process in order to write this book has been the hardest work of my heart. Sharing my story, I have been ever aware of the presence of each of my boys helping me to share authentic words to describe their mother's loss. I couldn't have done it without their permission and help. I have allowed my words to flow directly and freely from my heart, making me openly vulnerable. It is a risk I have accepted. My story has not been a pretty or a perfect one, but it is my story. Drawing strength from family and friends who have supported me, I don't take for granted the blessings of two beautiful daughters, Elizabeth and Ondrea, who add sparkle to our lives, along with our eight amazing grandchildren who will carry the light of hope forward in their lives.

Even in the darkest of times, hope is never gone. It is only hiding and is being held in the hands of lamp holders all around us who will hold our hope as long as needed, until we are ready to have them return it.

For now, I continue to learn what death has to teach me. I am learning mostly about living on. My battered heart is skillfully being repaired with a plethora of colorful threads painstakingly gathered on my grief journeys. I treasure each thread that strengthens me, and I trust that when the repair is done, its strong fiber will cause my changed heart to shimmer with joy and the light of hope that others can see even in their darkness.

Poems from a Mother's Heart

All poems by Judith Bond Maddock unless otherwise noted

Goodbye My Son

From my heart, from deep within
My love met you unaware.
It broke through shields of hurt and stone
To embrace your heart's despair.

My love cushioned and it molded you,
Never tiring, always giving.
The reflection of a small soul freed
Made my life so worth living.

Like a wounded bird you flew to me
As you settled within my nest.
You gasped my breath, all you could hold,
As I tried to give you rest.

There was no limit to the love
From my heart's hidden well it flowed,
As darkness lifted from your life
In your innocent eyes it showed.

Somewhere through those many years
Of incessant selfless giving,
My heart's well slowly went bone dry
And with it, joy for living.

As years have slipped into the past,
I've lost myself in you.
I've given till there's none for me,
Nothing more now I can do.

Would I reclaim all that I've given?
Not for a single minute!
For I can't imagine my life now,
Without you always in it.

But there comes a time in loving
When a mother must let go
With only hope and deepest prayers
That her gift of love will show.

My love will not be far away
You can trust it as you fly.
Someday you will come back to me...
Goodbye my son, goodbye.

His Eyes

Waiting in the lobby
My heart beating fast,
Where is this little boy
Who I'll finally meet at last?

As I peek down the hallway
I see a streak of blue.
And I wonder could it really be...
Could this finally be you?

With great anticipation
I wait to see a sign
Of the little boy I've yet to meet,
Though he seems already mine.

His eyes gazed up from a sea of brown
Framed big by glasses worn,
Those eyes so full of hope and fear
Showed a heart so often torn.

What could I do to stop their pain
And the lack of trust they showed?
No matter how I searched my soul,
I swear I didn't know.

Time passed by, as so it does,
And his eyes began to shine.
They started to reflect the love
When they looked back at mine.

Returning hope to this little heart
Became my mission strong,
And I prayed that God would help me
On those days when hope seemed gone.

Years later, now a handsome man,
As I look into his eyes
I only hope he truly knows
That a mother's love never dies.

I Flew with You

Where have you taken me...
That part of me that's no longer here?
Is that part that took flight with you
Feeling peace and is it again sure of heart?
Is it in a place called "HOPE"?
What are we seeing and feeling together?
Am I totally amazed at the wonder?
Are we held and bound by the veil of love,
Connected in completely unearthly ways?
Is there no presence of fear and pain, only the
boundless beauty of wholeness now?
A part of me flew with you—
Hold on and we'll fly through always to eternity,
Landing in a place called "HOPE".
Missing you forever,

Mom

Just One More Time

Call me Mom
Just one more time.
Let me hear your voice
Both pained and happy.
Let me hear your laugh
And see your big smile,
And tell you how much I admire
Your strength, how resilient you are –
So rich your hard-lived path had made you.

Let me know one more time
How much you appreciated me,
How much you knew you were loved,
And how hard we both tried.

Let me hear you tell me that we
Gave you complete love and the best life.
Give me one more Mother's Day card
Where you write I am "the best mom ever".

Let me hear one more time
About your dreams for tomorrow.
And let me believe you had to leave,
As on earth there was no lasting answer.

My Interpreter

At last, I have an interpreter,
I've given him to God's hand.
Jeffrey, please bring me clarity
To help me understand.

Help me learn how to accept
What now is and will be...
Knowing it cannot be changed,
That the change will be in me.

This world may have its beauty,
But none that will compare
To the peaceful paradise where you now dwell...
Void of struggles and illness there.

Your beautiful smile now brilliantly shines
Upon those you had to leave,
Restoring our hope by reminding us of
Your gift of acceptance as we grieve.

And so, I send my prayers
Of love and happiness to you.
I will still be your forever mom,
Each day sending love anew.

In the Beyond

In memory of my boys John Ryan, Joshua, and Jeffrey

I don't know where the Beyond might lie
Or where beloved souls might go.
It's a veiled mystery that human eyes can't see,
A quest of deep wondering…where can they be?
The deep bond of this mother's love so true
Yearns for the smiles and quirks that were you,
Grief rips right through me shattering my heart
With the pounding desperation of just knowing we're apart.
This is so much more than any mom should have to feel,
It's just so hard to believe that you are gone for real.
So many questions with no answers there to soothe me,
Left only with haunting visions that leave me lost and dreary.

Perhaps it's not my time to know
Their destination, when they go?
And that the love sent with them when they went away
Will carry them to paradise where they want to stay.

A place of no struggle and all absence of pain,
With a beauty of wholeness that here was in vain.
A place that doesn't take, but will only give
That brings total joy when they see where they live.
And maybe there is no need to understand,
But better to accept the will of God's hand,
And believe in God's power of love at its best
That leads us to put our faith to the test.
Death's mystery to understand our loss
May all come together at the foot of the cross,
When we come soul to soul and embrace in great love
Those we've missed here on earth now welcoming us above.

Holidays

Henry Wadsworth Longfellow

The holiest of all holidays are those
   Kept by ourselves in silence and apart;
   The secret anniversaries of the heart,
   When the full river of feeling overflows;

The happy days unclouded to their close;
   The sudden joys that out of darkness start
   As flames from ashes; swift desires that dart
   Like swallows singing down each wind that blows!

White as the gleam of a receding sail,
   White as a cloud that floats and fades in air,
   White as the whitest lily on a stream,

These tender memories are;—a Fairy Tale
   Of some enchanted land we know not where,
   But lovely as a landscape in a dream.

Made in the USA
Monee, IL
03 July 2023

38626902R00075